THE CHOCOLATE LOVER'S COOKBOOK

THE CHOCOLATE LOVER'S COOKBOOK

by Billie Little

Medallion Books   ꟽ   *Los Angeles*

THE CHOCOLATE LOVER'S COOKBOOK

Copyright © 1986 by Billie Little

All rights reserved, including the right to reproduce this book or portions thereof in any form.

An original Medallion Books edition, published for the first time anywhere.

First printing, July 1986

Book design by Robin Murawski
Cover typography by Jean-Louis Ginibre
Cover photograph by Brent Bear
Food and set styling by Edena Sheldon

Pine table, china plates, cup and saucer, antique pitcher, copper saucepan, and crockery mold courtesy of The Antique Guild, Los Angeles. Pottery pitcher and stemmed glassware courtesy of Faire La Cuisine, Malibu, California.

Recipes pictured (from left): Chocolate Rum Pie, Chunky Chocolate Chip Drops, Chocolate Fudge Cake, Creamy Chocolate Nog (foreground), Dark Russian Chocolate Cake, Fudge Brownies Divine, Chocolate Gingerbread Cookies, Rocky Road Pudding.

Library of Congress Cataloging-in-Publication Data

Little, Billie.
    The chocolate lover's cookbook.

    Includes index.
    1. Cookery (Chocolate) I. Title.
TX767.C5L58   1986   641.6'374   86-12634
ISBN 1-55627-008-9

The Medallion name and Medallion logotype are trademarks of Medallion Books, Inc.

MEDALLION BOOKS, INC.
5455 Wilshire Boulevard, Suite 1700
Los Angeles, California 90036

Printed in the United States of America

CONTENTS

ACKNOWLEDGMENTS

To my wonderful family, friends and neighbors who contributed their favorite chocolate recipes and helped taste and enjoy many of the recipes on the following pages, my grateful thanks. Very special thanks to Helen J. Britt, Director, Home Economics and Consumer Service of the Nestlé Company; Mrs. Pat Neville, Product Publicist of the General Foods Kitchens Company; Jeanne and Malcolm O. Campbell, Executive Vice Presidents of the Van Leer Chocolate Company; and Irma Hyams of the Chocolate Information Council, Chocolate Manufacturers Association of America. The companies whose products we have used are, of course, included in these acknowledgments. Credit also should go to my faithful typist, Marie Slavens, for deciphering!

Copies of the *Story of Chocolate* and additional information may be obtained from the Chocolate Manufacturers Association of America, 1812 K Street, N.W., Washington, D.C., 20006; the Chocolate Information Council of the Chocolate Manufacturers Association of U.S.A., 777 Third Avenue, New York, N.Y. 10017; the "Chocolate News", P.O. Box 1745, FDR Station, New York, N.Y., 10150; and *The Chocolate Bible* by Adrienne Marcus, The Putnam Publishing Group, 200 Madison Avenue, New York, N.Y. 10016.

PREFACE

Of all the flavors known, chocolate is the hands-down favorite! Prized not only for its flavor and texture, chocolate has long been recognized as a source of quick energy. Surveys have proven that students can improve their ability to do well on exams by increasing their intake of chocolate. History shows it was included in the diets of Queen Victoria's troops in the field as well as in the rations of soldiers in the Civil War, World War I, and World War II. Chocolate is still a standard in the rations of our armed forces today.

One of the most popular uses of chocolate, of course, is in the wonderful flavor it lends to desserts. Both a flavor and a food, it is a popular ingredient in cakes, cookies, drinks, custards, puddings, pastries, mousses, and sauces as well as in confectionery. It is the inspiration for famous recipes such as Black Bottom Pie, Parisienne Chocolate, Pots de Crème, the all-American favorite Chocolate Chip Cookies, and the famous Viennese Sachertorte.

There are so many who enjoy this flavor above all others that it seemed natural to collect my chocolate recipes into a book. This book is a compilation of wonderful chocolate recipes that I have used over the years and that I have avidly collected from relatives and friends. Once I started, I felt it would enhance the book to have newer recipes, and many of these have been contributed by the various chocolate companies who are included in my acknowledgments.

Years ago, cooks did not have available to them all the wonderful packaged materials that we have at our disposal today; this is particularly true of chocolate. Today we can purchase chocolate blancmange, chocolate cake mixes, chocolate candy mixes, chocolate frostings and puddings in a variety of forms at our grocery stores. These can be used as bases for innumerable dishes. With a little imagination, you will be able to come up with some delicious creations!

I hope you will enjoy these recipes as much as I have!

A FEW WORDS
ABOUT CHOCOLATE

If you have ever stopped to wonder a little about chocolate—where it comes from, what gives it its marvelous flavor—you are not alone! Even the most confirmed chocoholics among us have stopped consuming long enough to ponder the origins of and the stages that the bean goes through on the way to the finished product.

No one is really sure just where the first cocoa tree grew, but it is certain that it was either in Central or South America. As far as we know, the story of chocolate and the discovery of our country had their beginnings almost simultaneously. When Columbus returned to Spain after his discovery of America, among the many treasures he placed before the court of King Ferdinand were a few brown beans, which looked very much like almonds. King Ferdinand, however, did not have the vision to see how important these cocoa beans were to become.

It was not until Hernando Cortés, the Spanish explorer, saw the commercial possibilities, that cocoa beans became well known. In 1519 at Emperor Montezuma's court in Mexico, Cortés observed the Aztecs using the beans to prepare "chocolatl," the royal drink. Montezuma served this drink as though it were ambrosia fit for the gods. He served it to his Spanish guests in great, golden goblets. The Spaniards, however, found the taste to be much too bitter. To make it more palatable for Europeans, Cortés and his countrymen used cane sugar to sweeten it.

After Cortés brought the chocolate back to Spain, it underwent additional changes that increased its popularity—someone added cinnamon, another a bit of vanilla, and still another decided it would be more agreeable if it were served hot. Before long the Spanish aristocracy was boasting of the delectability of this drink; Spain rapidly established cocoa plantations in its overseas possessions, launching what was to become a very profitable business.

For nearly a hundred years, the Spaniards kept the art of cocoa production a secret from the rest of Europe, but eventually the secret leaked out through Spanish monks. Before long chocolate was being acclaimed throughout Europe as a delicious, health-giving food. It was served at the fashionable court of Louis XIII in France, where it was proclaimed *the* drink. Then, in 1657, word spread across the English Channel to London, and the first of many shops were opened where chocolate was sold at luxury prices. At first only the very wealthy were able to afford it. Its exclusiveness turned chocolate into such a fashionable drink that some of the shops became famous clubs, such as "The Cocoa Tree." But by 1730, as mass production replaced the manual methods of production common in small shops, the price had dropped to within reach of those less affluent.

The advent of the Industrial Revolution in the nineteenth century led to two more major developments in the chocolate industry. The first was the perfection of the steam engine, which was capable of handling the cocoa-grinding process. The second, in 1828, was the invention of the cocoa press. The cocoa press not only brought prices down, but also improved the quality of the beverage by squeezing out part of the cocoa butter, producing the flavor and smooth consistency we are accustomed to today.

The first chocolate factory in the United States was established in 1765 at Milton Lower Mills, near Dorchester, Massachusetts. Chocolate production there developed at a faster pace than in any other part of the world. It was the Swiss, however, who developed the first palatable solid, or "eating," chocolate. Around 1876 at Vevey, Switzerland, M. Daniel Peter perfected a process of making milk chocolate by combining the cocoa nib, sugar, cocoa butter and condensed milk.

WHAT IS CHOCOLATE?

Cocoa trees (evergreens) are found in many parts of the world—in West Africa: Ghana, Nigeria, The Ivory Coast and the Cameroons; in Latin America: Brazil, Colombia, Costa Rica, Ecuador, Mexico, Venezuela; and in Trinidad, the Dominican Republic, Sri Lanka, the Philippines, Samoa, the West Indies, and in other countries as well. The trees thrive only in moist, tropical climates, mainly within 20 degrees north or south of the Equator. There are as many varieties of cocoa trees as there are countries that grow them; the beans produced in each area have a distinctive flavor of their own. Generally, the chocolate we get is a blend of beans, selected for color, flavor and aroma or various other characteristics. The seeds, which are usually called *cocoa beans*, are the source of all chocolate and cocoa. The botanical term for the tree is *Theobroma cacao* or: "cocoa, food of the gods."

Inside each cocoa pod (the fruit) are the beans—between 20 to 40 in each pod. Shortly after the beans are exposed to air, their color changes from the original ivory to deep purple or lavender.

The next step in the transformation to edible chocolate, or cocoa, is fermentation. The fermenting of the pulp and the curing action taking place inside the bean at the same time are what give it the first hint of that wonderful aroma. When the beans have turned a rich, dark brown, they are ready to be dried. After the drying process, they are placed in sacks and carted to shipping centers to be sent to cocoa and chocolate factories all over the world.

Nibs, which contain an average of 53 percent cocoa butter, are the "meat" of the cocoa bean. These crisp, nutlike pieces result from the mechanical separation of the clean, roasted bean from its outer shell. The flavor of the chocolate depends on the quality of the nibs and the flavorings used, as well as a complex process of grinding, blending and heating. Roasting is done at controlled temperatures to bring out the full chocolate aroma and flavor.

Chocolate liquid, sometimes called "chocolate liquor," is the base material of all chocolate and cocoa products. Chocolate liquid is the result of grinding the nibs. The process generates sufficient heat to liquefy the cocoa butter so that the entire substance is transformed into a rich, brown mass—chocolate liquid. The liquor formed in an intermediate stage may be used in the confectionary trade, or the process may be continued and the resulting smooth mass of chocolate molded, cooled and packaged. It should be hard enough to snap when broken and be free of all signs of gritty, coarse particles. It gives off an aromatic smell and flavor as well as a rich, dark color.

Cocoa butter is a unique yellowish-white vegetable fat. Removed from the chocolate liquid under high pressure, it rarely turns rancid and has many uses. In addition to being an important ingredient in candies and confections, it is a component of many fine complexion creams, pomades, soaps and lotions.

Bitter chocolate, sometimes referred to as unsweetened, baking or cooking chocolate, is chocolate liquid that has been cooled and molded into blocks. Also available is a substitute for bitter chocolate that consists of cocoa and cocoa butter or vegetable fats in a semiliquid form. It is packaged in one-ounce envelopes sold by the box.

Cocoa powder is a general term for the portion of chocolate liquid that remains after most of the cocoa butter has been removed. The term includes breakfast cocoa, medium and low fat cocoas, and Dutch process cocoa.

Dutch process cocoa is cocoa powder that has been treated with alkali to neutralize the natural acids. Dutch process cocoa (which has nothing to do with the Netherlands) is darker in color, and the flavor is slightly mellower than that of natural cocoa.

Breakfast cocoa is cocoa powder with at least 22 percent cocoa butter.

Ready-to-use cocoa is a mixture of cocoa powder, sweetening, and other flavorings.

Sweet chocolate, which is also identified as semisweet, is prepared by blending chocolate liquid with varying amounts of sweetening and added cocoa butter. Flavorings may be included. After processing, the chocolate is cooled and is usually molded into bars. Semisweet chocolate is also available in bar form, but most popularly as pieces. Sweet and semisweet chocolate may be eaten as is or used as an ingredient in cakes, cookies, and frostings.

Milk chocolate is the most familiar kind of eating chocolate. It is made by combining chocolate liquid, extra cocoa butter, milk or cream, sweetening and flavorings. Milk chocolate is usually molded into bars and may contain raisins, nuts, and cream fillings.

Chocolate syrup is a combination of chocolate or cocoa flavoring, sweetening, water, salt and other flavorings.

Chocolate sauce is essentially the same as chocolate syrup, but heavier in density as a result of the addition of milk, cream, and/or butter.

White chocolate is a substance erroneously called chocolate since it contains no chocolate liquid and therefore does not comply with government standards for chocolate. Correctly called "confectioners" coating, it may be made with vegetable fats instead of cocoa butter, may be tinted with vegetable coloring, and may contain added flavors.

COOKING WITH CHOCOLATE

In order to enjoy the wonderful flavor, nutritional qualities and textures to the maximum, cook chocolate with care. Chocolate can be melted either dry, in the top of a double boiler over simmering water, or in liquid. Either way, use low heat since chocolate scorches easily. Always cool the melted chocolate gradually.

Dry melting: Always be sure the bowl and spoon or spatula are absolutely dry. (Stir chocolate often for smooth, even consistency.) Cook over hot, but not boiling water, to avoid any rising steam. If even a drop of condensed moisture falls into the melting chocolate, it will stiffen and be almost impossible to use. If this should happen, however, you can rescue the chocolate. Stir in 1 to 2 tablespoons of vegetable shortening (*not* butter, since it contains moisture) until chocolate becomes fluid again. To melt a small quantity—1 to 2 ounces—wrap chocolate in aluminum foil and place in a warm spot on the stove.

Melting in liquid: Place chocolate in a large amount of liquid in a saucepan and melt over direct, low heat. (The recipe should call for at least ¼ cup liquid—juice, water, milk or spirits—to 6 ounces of chocolate.) Stir constantly, melting chocolate and liquid to blend thoroughly. When adding liquids to melted chocolate, be sure to add 2 or more tablespoons of the liquid at a time; otherwise the chocolate will stiffen and will not blend.

SUBSTITUTIONS

Although the recipes in this book have been developed for specific types of chocolate, in an emergency it is possible to make substitutions. If you find that you don't have the type of chocolate called for in a particular recipe, try the suggested substitutions that follow:

For 1 ounce (1 square) unsweetened chocolate, *substitute*

3 tablespoons unsweetened cocoa powder plus 1 tablespoon shortening or cooking oil.

For semisweet chocolate squares, *substitute*
semisweet chocolate chips as follows:

> **1 ounce (1 square) = 3 tablespoons chips**
> **2 ounces (2 squares) = ⅓ cup chips**
> **3 ounces (3 squares) = ½ cup chips**
> **4 ounces (4 squares) = ⅔ cup chips**
> **6 ounces (6 squares) = 1   cup chips**

For 1 square (1 ounce) of semisweet chocolate, *substitute*
1 square (1 ounce) unsweetened chocolate plus 1 tablespoon sugar.
For 6 squares (6 ounces) semisweet chocolate, *substitute*
6 tablespoons unsweetened cocoa powder plus ¼ cup sugar and ¼ cup shortening.

STORING CHOCOLATE

Always store chocolate in a cool (never warmer than 78° F), dry place. When a storage area is too hot, the cocoa butter in chocolate softens and rises to the surface, where it forms a gray film known as "bloom." Chocolate with bloom is safe to eat, but it may not taste very creamy or look very appetizing. Use it for melting down or baking.

All chocolate may be refrigerated, but be sure to seal it tightly so it doesn't take on odors or moisture from other foods. Refrigerated chocolate is always very hard and brittle. Allow it to return to room temperature before nibbling at it, if you value your teeth.

Chocolate may also be frozen for as long as 3 to 4 months without change in flavor, texture, or appearance.

The best conditions for storing cocoa are in a tightly sealed container at temperatures of 60 to 70° F and at 50 to 65 percent relative humidity. Cocoa tends to lump and lose its rich brown color if exposed to high temperature or humidity. Flavor is not affected, but the cocoa looks less appetizing.

For storing either chocolate or cocoa products, the ideal container material is glass. It protects the chocolate and won't absorb odors. An extra advantage is that it lets you see when you're running low.

Time Limits for Storing Chocolate Safely

Type of Chocolate	Pantry	Refrigerator	Freezer
Baking	2 years	2 years	5 years
Semisweet	1 year	2 years	5 years
Milk	6 months	1 year	2 years

MAKING CHOCOLATE
GARNISHES AND DECORATIONS

Chocolate may be grated, shredded, curled, or chopped for decorative purposes as well as for cooking or to speed up melting. Whatever the process or purpose, here are a few basic rules to follow for best results.

1. Handle the chocolate as little as possible.
2. Be sure your implements are absolutely dry.
3. If not using immediately, refrigerate the chocolate to prevent lumping together.

To curl: Use a vegetable peeler with a long narrow blade. Warm chocolate and blade slightly. Draw peeler along smooth surface of a chunk or bar of chocolate. For large curls pull the peeler over a wide surface of the chocolate; for small ones, pull the blade along a narrow side.

To grate: The chocolate must be cool and firm. Use a hand grater or a rotary type with a hand crank. (Clean often so chocolate doesn't clog grating surface.) A blender can also be used, but be sure to cut the chocolate into small pieces.

To shred: Use a large piece of cool, firm chocolate and shave with a vegetable or potato peeler.

To chop: Place the chocolate on a wooden cutting board and use a sharp heavy knife or cleaver.

HOW TO USE THIS BOOK

Follow these suggestions to get the best results from the recipes in this book.

- ALWAYS READ THE RECIPE THROUGH. Turn on oven to correct temperature called for in recipe.
- Assemble all ingredients and allow to reach room temperature (about 72°F) before commencing recipe.
- Be sure baking pans are prepared according to size and instructions in recipe.
- Always use standard measuring cups and spoons.
- Sift flour before measuring, then spoon it gently into the measuring cup and level it off. Sift it again when specified with other dry ingredients.
- When measuring by spoonfuls, put the measuring spoon into the ingredient, then level off.
- Brown sugar should be firmly packed into proper measuring cup.
- When measuring shortening into a cup, be sure no air spaces are left and it is leveled off.
- Be sure the measuring cup is on a level surface when measuring liquids. Pour in the liquid until it reaches correct level.
- If you prefer nonfat dry milk, be sure to read instructions on box. If the recipe calls for 1 cup of milk, use 3 tablespoons of dry milk with dry ingredients and then use 1 cup water as the liquid. If using liquefied dry milk, substitute it for equal amounts of regular milk.
- Place the rack in middle of the oven when you are ready to bake; set pans in the middle of the rack, away from the sides and rear of oven.
- To determine if a cake is done, insert a cake tester into the center of the cake (it will come out clean when the cake is done) or press the center of the cake very lightly with your finger tips; if no imprint is left, the cake is done.
- When cooling a butter cake, place the pan on a wire rack for 5 to 6 minutes, then loosen the cake from the sides of the pan. Remove the cake from the pan. Complete the cooling process on a wire rack.
- For cooling chiffon, sponge, and angel food cakes, let the cake pan hang inverted on the neck of a wine bottle until cool. Then loosen the cake from the sides of the pan with spatula and remove it carefully.
- When baking instructions for a chocolate cake or cookies call for greasing and flouring the pan, add a little unsweetened cocoa to the flour. The finished cake or cookies won't have that floury look.

CHAPTER ONE

BEVERAGES

Hot Beverages

BREAKFAST CHOCOLATE

A hearty accompaniment to breakfast.
Makes 5 to 6 servings

4 cups milk
2 ounces (2 squares) unsweetened
  chocolate, melted
2 egg yolks

3 tablespoons sugar
½ cup whipping cream, whipped

Heat milk. Gradually add chocolate, stirring until dissolved. When completely dissolved, remove from heat. Beat egg yolks with sugar; stir into chocolate. Return mixture to heat and scald. Serve hot with dollop of whipped cream on top.

CHOCOLATE CHIP DRINK

Quick, basic hot chocolate.
Makes 4 servings

4 cups hot milk
6 ounces (1 cup) semisweet
  chocolate chips, melted

½ teaspoon vanilla extract
1 cup whipped cream (optional)

Pour milk over melted chocolate. Add vanilla; stir well. Beat with rotary beater until chocolate dissolves. Add dollop of whipped cream if desired.

RICH HOT CHOCOLATE

Makes 6 servings

6 ounces (1 cup) semisweet
  chocolate chips
1 cup water
¹⁄₁₆ teaspoon salt

1½ cups milk
1½ cups whipping cream
1 teaspoon vanilla extract

Melt chocolate chips with water and salt over medium heat. Blend well. Bring to a boil, stirring constantly. Place in top of double boiler; add milk and whipping cream. Heat to scalding. Beat with rotary beater until foamy. Serve immediately.

•

MEXICAN CHOCOLATE

Cinnamon adds a distinctive Mexican flavor.
Makes 2 servings

2 cups milk
¼ teaspoon cinnamon
2 ounces sweet chocolate, coarsely
chopped

¼ cup whipping cream, whipped

Heat milk and cinnamon until scalded. Add chopped chocolate and stir until melted. Remove from heat. Beat with electric mixer until frothy and well blended. Pour into cups. Top with dollop of whipped cream.

•

ANGELA'S MEXICAN CHOCOLATE

A slightly richer version of basic Mexican chocolate.
Makes 7 to 8 servings

4 ounces (4 squares) unsweetened
chocolate
½ cup boiling water
6 tablespoons sugar
4 cups milk, scalded
2 cups whipping cream
¼ teaspoon salt

⅛ teaspoon nutmeg
⅛ teaspoon allspice
2 teaspoons cinnamon
2 eggs
2 teaspoons vanilla extract
½ cup whipping cream, whipped

Grate chocolate in top of double boiler over boiling water; add ½ cup boiling water. When chocolate is melted beat with wooden spoon until smooth. Stir in sugar, milk, whipping cream, salt and spices. Cook 30 minutes, beating vigorously every 8 or 10 minutes. When ready to serve, beat eggs with vanilla. Add a little of the hot chocolate to eggs. Stir remainder of chocolate into mix and beat vigorously 3 to 4 minutes. Serve at once in preheated mugs with dollop of whipped cream on top.

•

MAKING HOT CHOCOLATE AND COCOA

Always cook milk over a very low flame or in the top of a double boiler, otherwise a skin will form. Slow cooking will also prevent settling—the formation of a dark layer at the bottom of the cup or pan after the drink has stood for a while. Take a lead from the Aztecs: before serving beat any hot chocolate drink with a molinillo, if you happen to have one on hand. If not, a rotary beater will do. Beating minimizes settling and brings out the chocolate flavor.

PARISIENNE CHOCOLATE

French-style instant hot chocolate.
Makes 16 servings

2½ ounces (2½ squares) semisweet chocolate
½ cup cold water
½ teaspoon salt

¾ cup sugar
½ cup whipping cream, whipped
Scalded milk

Cut chocolate into pieces. Add to water and cook, stirring constantly until smooth and thick. Remove from heat; add salt and sugar. Cook 4 to 5 minutes, stirring constantly. Cool. Fold in whipped cream. Store in refrigerator. Use 1 tablespoon to a cup. Fill with scalded milk. Serve at once.

VIENNA CHOCOLATE COFFEE DRINK

Delicately flavored with cloves and cinnamon.
Makes 8 servings

8 whole cloves
3 sticks cinnamon
½ cup instant coffee
¼ cup cocoa

2 quarts boiling water
½ cup sugar
1 cup whipping cream, whipped
Cinnamon

Tie whole cloves and cinnamon sticks in a cheesecloth and place in large saucepan with instant coffee and cocoa. Add boiling water and cover. Steep 5 to 6 minutes. Remove spices and stir in sugar. Pour into thick glasses. Top with dollop of whipped cream and sprinkle of cinnamon.

ANNE'S HOT CHOCOLATE

Makes 6 servings

3 cups milk
½ cup chocolate-flavored drink mix
1 pint orange sherbet

Whipped cream or whipped
  imitation cream topping

Mix milk and drink mix. Stir over medium heat until hot; do not boil. Stir in sherbet until completely melted; reheat. Pour into serving mugs. Garnish with chosen topping.

CHOCOLATE PEANUT QUICKY

Hot chocolate with a new twist.
Makes 2 servings

¼ cup prepared instant chocolate
1 tablespoon creamy-style peanut
  butter
1½ cups milk

1 tablespoon sugar
¼ teaspoon vanilla extract
¼ cup whipping cream, whipped

Stir all ingredients together. Bring to a boil over medium heat, stirring constantly. Remove from heat. Beat well. Pour into cups. Top with dollop of whipped cream.

EUROPEAN COFFEE-CHOCOLATE DRINK

Coffee flavored and creamy.
Makes 4 to 5 servings

1 egg white
½ cup whipping cream
½ teaspoon vanilla extract
1½ cups hot coffee

2 tablespoons cocoa
4 tablespoons sugar
1/16 teaspoon salt

Beat egg white until stiff. Whip cream until stiff and fold in vanilla, then fold whipped cream into egg white. Fill coffee cups about ¼ full with cream mixture. Mix coffee, cocoa, sugar and salt. Pour over cream mixture in cups. Serve at once.

SPICED COCOA

Ideal for a chilly afternoon.
Makes 8 servings

½ cup cocoa
½ cup sugar
¹⁄₁₆ teaspoon salt
⅛ teaspoon allspice

4 cups water
2½ cups evaporated milk
1 teaspoon vanilla extract
½ cup whipping cream, whipped

Mix cocoa, sugar, salt and allspice. Add water and bring to a boil; boil 3 minutes. Add milk. Reheat. Beat with rotary beater until frothy; add vanilla. Garnish with dollop of whipped cream.

•

SAN FRANCISCO GROG

Makes 8 to 10 servings

6 cinnamon sticks
2 teaspoons whole cloves
½ cup sugar
¼ cup chocolate syrup
½ teaspoon rum flavoring
½ teaspoon brandy flavoring
½ teaspoon vanilla extract

2 quarts hot coffee, double
   strength
¹⁄₁₆ teaspoon salt
½ cup whipping cream, whipped
1 orange peel, cut in strips
   (garnish)
1 lemon peel, cut in strips (garnish)

Combine all ingredients except orange and lemon peel and whipping cream in chafing dish. Steep about 15 minutes over very low heat; do not boil. Serve in small mugs with a dollop of whipped cream and a twist of peel on top.

•

CHOCOLATE CAFÉ ROYALE

Serve with or instead of dessert.
Makes 1 serving

1 teaspoon instant coffee
½ teaspoon cocoa
½ tablespoon sugar

½ cup hot water
1 ounce brandy

Place coffee, cocoa and sugar in a demitasse. Fill halfway with hot water. Stir to dissolve sugar, cocoa and coffee; add brandy at lip of cup so that it drizzles down side to float on mixture. Ignite with match. Stir to extinguish flame.

·

HOLIDAY CHOCOLATE DRINK

Makes 6 to 7 servings

3 ounces (½ cup) semisweet
  chocolate chips
¹⁄₁₆ teaspoon salt
¼ teaspoon cinnamon
1 cup sherry

3 cups milk
½ cup whipping cream
1 teaspoon vanilla extract
½ cup whipping cream, whipped
  Nutmeg (garnish)

Place chocolate chips, salt, cinnamon and sherry in top of double boiler. Cook over hot water until chocolate melts, stirring constantly. Heat milk and whipping cream until it comes to scalding point; add to chocolate mixture. Beat until foamy; add vanilla. Pour into cups and top with dollop of whipped cream. Sprinkle with nutmeg.

·

NEW ROCHELLE NIFTY

Makes 2 servings

3 tablespoons instant cocoa mix
1 tablespoon instant coffee
1 cup water, boiling

½ teaspoon flavoring of choice
  (vanilla, almond, rum)
½ cup whipping cream, whipped

Mix well all ingredients except whipping cream in shaker. Pour into large glasses and top with dollops of whipped cream.

·

CHOCOLATE COFFEE LIQUEUR

Makes 3 to 4 servings

2 cups coffee, double strength
1 ounce (1 square) unsweetened
  chocolate
½ teaspoon rum flavoring
½ teaspoon brandy flavoring

1½ teaspoons coffee liqueur
⅛ cup sugar
¼ cup whipping cream, whipped

Heat coffee and chocolate, stirring until chocolate melts. Add rum and brandy flavorings, liqueur and sugar. Heat thoroughly. Serve hot, topped with dollops of whipped cream.

CHOCOLATE DIABLO CAFÉ

A heady, elegant brew.
Makes 3 servings

3 tablespoons brandy flavoring
1½ tablespoons anisette
1½ tablespoons Cointreau
½ small orange, peeled in strips
½ small lemon, peeled in strips
1 3-inch stick cinnamon

4 or 5 cloves
4 cubes sugar
2 tablespoons chocolate syrup
2 cups coffee, double strength
½ cup whipping cream, whipped

Heat brandy in chafing dish and as soon as it is warm, ignite it. Slowly add Cointreau and anisette; allow some of alcohol to burn off. Add remaining ingredients, except cream. Steep without simmering about 15 minutes. Serve in demitasse cups. Garnish with spoonfuls of whipped cream.

CHOCOLATE ICE CREAM CUP

Makes 6 to 7 servings

¼ cup instant coffee
2 tablespoons sugar
2 cups water

¼ cup rum
½ teaspoon vanilla extract
⅔ cup chocolate ice cream, softened

Dissolve coffee and sugar in water. Add rum, vanilla and ice cream; stir until smooth. Heat. Serve in demitasse cups.

Cold Beverages

CHOCOLATE SODA

The classic chocolate soda.
Makes 1 serving

1 generous scoop of vanilla or
chocolate ice cream

2 tablespoons chocolate syrup
Carbonated water

Place ice cream and chocolate syrup in a tall glass. Fill with carbonated water.

•

COFFEE DRINK

Makes 6 servings

2 ounces (2 squares) bitter
chocolate
1 cup whipping cream
2 cups coffee, double strength
¾ cup sugar
1 teaspoon vanilla extract

½ teaspoon almond extract
1 pint chocolate ice cream
1 cup whipping cream, whipped

Dissolve chocolate and whipping cream over hot water in top of double boiler. Stir until chocolate dissolves; add sugar and coffee. Cool and add vanilla and almond extracts. Put chocolate ice cream in bowl of mixer. Pour coffee-chocolate mixture over and beat until completely blended. Pour into tall glasses. Serve at once, garnished with dollop of whipped cream on top of each.

•

BLACK COW

A new classic soda.
Makes 1 serving

1 scoop chocolate ice cream

Root beer

Place 1 scoop chocolate ice cream in a tall glass; fill glass with root beer.

MOCHA PUNCH

Makes 1 serving

1 large scoop chocolate ice cream
Cold coffee, double strength

Whipped cream
Nutmeg (garnish)

Place 1 large scoop chocolate ice cream in a tall glass. Fill glass with cold coffee. Top with spoonful of whipped cream and sprinkle with nutmeg.

.

CHOCOLATE SPICE SHAKE

A rich dessert drink, spiced with nutmeg.
Makes 4 servings

4 egg yolks
4 cups milk, chilled
½ cup Cocoa Malt (see following
   recipe)

⅛ teaspoon nutmeg
½ cup whipping cream, whipped
½ cup chocolate chips (garnish)

Beat egg yolks and add chilled milk. Add Cocoa Malt and beat with rotary beater until dissolved. Flavor with nutmeg and pour into large glasses. Place a dollop of whipped cream on top of each, topped with chocolate chips.

COCOA MALT

Makes 1 serving

2 tablespoons Cocoa Malt
2 tablespoons cold milk

½ cup hot milk

Blend Cocoa Malt and 2 tablespoons cold milk together. Add hot milk and stir until dissolved. Serve hot or cold.

.

CHOCOLATE MOCHA COOLER

A sophisticated, afternoon cooler.
Makes 2 servings

2 tablespoons chocolate syrup
½ teaspoon instant coffee

¼ cup rum

Mix all ingredients in shaker. Pour into tall glasses filled with cracked ice.

CREAMY CHOCOLATE NOG

A dash of orange extract adds a special touch.
Makes 3 servings

1 **egg, separated**
2 **tablespoons sugar**
1¼ **cups milk**
⅓ **cup prepared instant chocolate**
  drink

½ **cup whipping cream, whipped**
⅛ **teaspoon orange extract**

Beat egg white until stiff but not dry. Gradually beat in sugar until stiff and glossy. Beat milk, instant drink and egg yolk until well mixed. Blend in whipped cream, egg white mixture and orange extract. Pour into glasses.

●

HACIENDA DELIGHT

Makes 3 servings

1 **teaspoon instant coffee**
1 **tablespoon boiling water**
1 **scoop chocolate ice cream**

⅓ **cup crème de cacao**
1 **teaspoon clear crème de menthe**
1 **cup crushed ice**

Dissolve instant coffee in boiling water. Combine all ingredients; shake well in shaker or blend at high speed of blender about a minute. Serve in glasses.

●

MOCHA CHOCOLATE FLOAT

Try this as a do-ahead luncheon dessert drink
Makes 6 servings

2 **ounces (2 squares) unsweetened**
  chocolate
½ **cup sugar**
1 **cup hot coffee, double strength**

4 **cups milk, scalded**
½ **cup whipping cream, whipped**

Melt chocolate in a large saucepan; add sugar and dissolve. Add coffee, stirring constantly. Add scalded milk and blend. Cook 10 to 15 minutes until smooth. Remove from heat; cool. Pour into dessert glasses and refrigerate. Top with whipped cream before serving.

CHOCOLATE RUM DRINK

Makes 4 servings

3 *cups chocolate ice cream*
2 *cups club soda, chilled*
4 *tablespoons chocolate syrup*

¼ *cup whipping cream*
2 *teaspoons vanilla extract*
¼ *cup Jamaican rum*

Combine ingredients in shaker. Cover and shake until foamy.

·

CHOCOLATE ESPRESSO DESSERT DRINK

A delicious chocolate "cocktail."
Makes 4 servings

½ *cup gin*
½ *cup crème de café*
4 *tablespoons cold coffee*

½ *cup chocolate ice cream, softened*
6 *tablespoons powdered sugar*
12 *ice cubes, crushed*

Place all ingredients in blender. Blend at high speed until smooth. Pour into glasses.

·

SAVORY CHOCOLATE

Makes 12 servings

1 *egg white*
3 *tablespoons sugar*
1½ *cups sweetened cocoa*
3 *quarts milk*

¾ *teaspoon peppermint extract*
½ *teaspoon vanilla extract*
1 *cup whipping cream, whipped*

Dip rims of tall glasses into egg white, then into sugar. Chill glasses until rim has set. Mix cocoa, milk and vanilla and peppermint extracts. Pour into glasses. Garnish each with dollop of whipped cream.

·

PENINSULA FLOAT

Makes 1 serving

1 **teaspoon instant coffee**
2 **tablespoons marshmallow cream**
1 **scoop chocolate ice cream,**
   softened

½ **cup cold milk**
¼ **teaspoon almond extract**
¼ **teaspoon vanilla extract**

Place all ingredients in glass. Stir until ice cream is partially dissolved.

·

CHOCOLATE
BRANDY DESSERT DRINK

Impress guests with this stylish, warm-weather dessert drink.
Makes 7 to 8 servings

¾ **cup sugar**
¾ **cup cocoa**
1 **quart milk**
2 **cups coffee, double strength**

1 **teaspoon rum flavoring**
1 **cup brandy**
1 **cup whipping cream, whipped**

Mix sugar and cocoa; stir in milk gradually, making a smooth paste. Heat until boiling; remove from heat. Add coffee and rum flavoring; chill about 3 hours. Add brandy and mix well. Fill glasses about ¾ full. Place a dollop of whipped cream on top of each.

·

CHAPTER TWO

COOKIES

Bar Cookies

CHOCOLATE WALNUT BARS

Amazingly quick!
Makes 32

1 cup canned chocolate frosting
1 cup flour
2 eggs

½ cup butter, softened
½ teaspoon vanilla extract
1 cup walnuts, chopped

Preheat oven to 350°. Grease a 9 × 13-inch pan. Blend all ingredients until thoroughly mixed. Spread batter in pan. Bake until tester inserted in center comes out clean, about 30 minutes. Cool a few minutes in pan. Cut into bars.

■

ANN'S CHOCOLATE BARS

Makes 42

½ cup butter
1 cup sugar
1 egg
2 tablespoons milk

2 cups flour, sifted
¼ teaspoon salt
2½ ounces (2½ squares) unsweetened
  chocolate, melted

Preheat oven to 400°. Cream butter and sugar; add egg. Add milk and flour alternately. Mix in chocolate. Fill a cookie press. Form cookies on ungreased cookie sheets. Bake until lightly browned, 8 to 10 minutes, being careful not to burn.

■

CHOCOLATE FUDGE CREAM BARS

Cream cheese adds flavor and density to these easy fudge bars.
Makes about 20

1 cup canned chocolate frosting
1 egg
1 cup cream cheese, softened

¼ cup flour
½ teaspoon black walnut flavoring

Preheat oven to 375°. Grease an 8-inch square pan. Blend all ingredients together until well mixed. Beat at high speed of mixer until cream cheese is smooth, about 1 minute. Pour into pan. Bake until tester inserted in center of pan comes out clean, about 45 minutes. Cool; cut into 1½ × 2-inch bars.

·

FROSTED CHOCOLATE
MOCHA RUM NUT SQUARES

Rich rum- and coffee-flavored squares with a light chocolate frosting.
Makes about 54

1 cup unsalted butter
2 cups sugar
4 ounces (4 squares) unsweetened
  chocolate, melted
4 eggs
1½ cups flour
1/16 teaspoon salt

1 teaspoon vanilla extract
½ teaspoon black walnut flavoring
½ cup coffee, double strength
1/8 cup rum
1 cup nuts, chopped
Lightweight Chocolate Frosting
  (see following recipe)

Preheat oven to 325°. Grease a 9 × 13-inch pan, line with waxed paper and grease again. Cream butter and sugar; add melted chocolate. Stir in eggs one at a time, beating after each addition. Add flour, salt, vanilla and black walnut flavoring. Fold in nuts. Bake until tester inserted in center comes out clean, about 35 minutes. Cool 10 minutes. Cut into 1½-inch squares. Remove from pan. When completely cool, frost with Lightweight Chocolate Frosting.

LIGHTWEIGHT
CHOCOLATE FROSTING

Makes about 1 cup

½ cup unsalted butter, softened
3 ounces (3 squares) semisweet
  chocolate, melted
3½ cups powdered sugar
1 teaspoon rum

1 teaspoon vanilla extract
1 teaspoon almond extract
1 egg white
1/16 teaspoon salt
1 to 2 tablespoons whipping cream

Blend softened butter with sugar, rum and vanilla and almond extracts. Add melted chocolate, unbeaten egg white and salt; mix well. Add sufficient whipping cream to reach spreading consistency.

·

QUICK MILK CHOCOLATE FROSTING

Need a quick method for frosting cookies or small cakes? Use milk chocolate bars. Place small pieces of milk chocolate on cookies or cakes hot from the oven. Cover lightly with aluminum foil and leave for a few minutes until the chocolate softens. Then spread evenly or swirl with a small spatula. Let stand until chocolate is firm.

CHOCOLATE PECAN BARS

Makes 6 dozen

12 ounces (2 cups) semisweet
   chocolate chips
½ cup butter
¾ cup sugar
2 eggs

2 cups flour, sifted
¼ teaspoon salt
2 teaspoons hot water
1 cup pecans, finely chopped

Preheat oven to 325°. Melt chocolate chips and butter in a double boiler over hot, not boiling, water; remove from water. Blend in ¼ cup sugar and eggs, one at a time; beat well. Stir in flour. Spread in 10 × 15 × 1-inch ungreased pan. Make topping by mixing nuts, ½ cup sugar, water and salt; sprinkle over batter. Bake 20 minutes. Cool. Cut into 1 × 2-inch bars.

FROSTED FUDGE BARS

Makes 16

1 cup flour
¼ teaspoon baking powder
¼ teaspoon salt
2 ounces (2 squares) unsweetened
   chocolate
½ cup butter
2 eggs

1 cup sugar
½ teaspoon vanilla extract
1 cup nuts, finely chopped
   Special Frosting (see following
     recipe)
½ cup nuts, chopped (garnish)

Preheat oven to 350°. Grease an 8-inch square pan. Mix and sift together flour, baking powder and salt. Melt chocolate and butter. Beat eggs. Gradually add sugar, stirring constantly. Add chocolate mixture and vanilla. Beat 1 minute, then add sifted dry ingredients. Blend well. Stir in nuts. Place in pan. Bake until top is dry, about 35 minutes. Cool. Spread with Special Frosting; sprinkle with chopped nuts. When set, cut into bars about 1 × 4 inches.

SPECIAL FROSTING

Makes about ½ cup

2 ounces (2 squares) unsweetened
 chocolate
¼ cup sugar

3 tablespoons water
½ teaspoon vanilla extract

Melt chocolate in top of double boiler over hot water. Mix sugar and water in saucepan; stir over medium heat until sugar dissolves. Boil 1 minute. Pour slowly into chocolate, stirring constantly. Beat until thick; add vanilla. Blend well before spreading over cookies or bars.

■

OATMEAL-PECAN FUDGE BARS

Crunchy, blond bars with a thick chocolate and pecan layer.
Makes 4 dozen

½ teaspoon baking soda
½ teaspoon salt
¾ cup flour, sifted
 1 cup brown sugar, firmly packed
½ cup plus 1 tablespoon butter
1½ teaspoons vanilla extract
 1 egg

1 cup cornflakes, finely crushed
1 cup rolled oats (quick cooking)
1½ cup pecans, chopped
⅓ cup sweetened condensed milk
6 ounces (1 cup) semisweet
 chocolate chips
¼ teaspoon salt

Preheat oven to 350°. Grease a 9-inch square pan. Sift together first three ingredients; set aside. Combine brown sugar, all but 1 tablespoon butter and ½ teaspoon vanilla; beat until creamy. Blend in flour mixture slowly. Stir in cornflakes, rolled oats and ½ cup pecans. Remove a cup of dough, packed firm, and put aside. Place remaining dough in pan. Melt chocolate chips and remaining butter; remove from heat. Add 1 cup pecans, condensed milk, 1 teaspoon vanilla and salt; blend well. Press evenly over cookie mixture. Crumble remaining dough over top. Bake 30 minutes. Cool. Cut into 1 × 1½-inch bars.

■

AUNT IRMA'S CHOCOLATE SQUARES

Topped with a layer of marshmallows and a rich, dark icing.
Makes 2 dozen

½ *cup butter*	1 *teaspoon vanilla extract*
1 *cup sugar*	3 *ounces (3 squares) unsweetened*
4 *eggs*	*chocolate, melted*
½ *cup flour*	32 *marshmallows*
1 *cup nuts, coarsely broken*	*Auntie's Fudge Icing (see*
¼ *teaspoon cinnamon*	*following recipe)*

Preheat oven to 350°. Grease a 8 × 12 × 2-inch biscuit pan. Cream sugar and butter together; add eggs. Beat well. Add flour, nuts, and cinnamon. Stir in vanilla and chocolate. Place in pan. Bake until tester inserted in center of cake comes out clean, about 20 minutes. When done, lay marshmallows on top and return to oven with heat off and door open for 5 minutes. When cold, ice in the pan with Auntie's Fudge Icing. When completely cold, cut into 2-inch squares.

AUNTIE'S FUDGE ICING

Makes 1¼ cups

1¼ *cups cocoa*	1 *teaspoon vinegar*
2½ *cups sugar*	1 *teaspoon vanilla extract*
1 *cup milk*	½ *cup marshmallow cream*
¼ *cup butter*	

Mix first four ingredients in top of double boiler over boiling water until chocolate melts. Stir in vinegar and vanilla. Add marshmallow cream.

·

CHOCOLATE KRISPIE PEANUT LOGS

Makes 3 dozen

4½ *ounces (¾ cup) semisweet*	4 *cups Cocoa Krispies cereal*
chocolate chips	1 *teaspoon vanilla extract*
⅓ *cup peanut butter*	

Butter a 9 × 9 × 2-inch pan. Melt chocolate chips with peanut butter over low heat, stirring until well blended. Remove from heat. Add cereal; stir until well coated with chocolate mixture. Press into pan. Refrigerate until firm. Cut into bars 3 × ¾ inches.

■

CHOCOLATE NUT TREE COOKIES
Makes 6 to 8

¾ *cup flour*
½ *teaspoon baking powder*
¼ *teaspoon salt*
 2 *ounces (2 squares) unsweetened*
   chocolate
½ *cup unsalted butter, softened*

2 *eggs*
1 *cup sugar*
1 *teaspoon vanilla extract*
½ *teaspoon almond extract*
1 *cup sliced nuts*

Preheat oven to 350°. Line bottoms of two 8-inch cake pans with waxed paper, then grease paper and sides of pans. Sift together dry ingredients. Melt chocolate with butter over low heat. Beat eggs and sugar until light and fluffy; stir in chocolate mixture. Add dry ingredients and vanilla and almond extracts, mixing well. Fold in ½ cup nuts. Turn batter, dividing evenly, into pans. Sprinkle with remaining nuts (¼ cup for each pan). Bake until tester inserted in center comes out clean, about 20 minutes. Cool 10 minutes in pans. Invert onto wire racks and remove waxed paper. Cut into pie-shaped wedges with sharp knife. When cool, stand in form of a tree on tiered dish.

■

CHOCOLATE CRANBERRY BARS
Makes 32

 4 *ounces sweet chocolate*
 2 *cups flour, sifted*
¾ *teaspoon cinnamon*
¾ *teaspoon ginger*
¼ *teaspoon allspice*
½ *teaspoon ground cloves*
½ *teaspoon baking powder*

1 *cup butter*
⅓ *cup sugar*
2 *eggs*
½ *cup whole-berry cranberry sauce*
¾ *cup buttermilk*
  Icing (optional)

Preheat oven to 350°. Grease and flour a 9 × 13-inch pan. Melt chocolate over low heat, stirring constantly. Cool. Sift together flour, spices and baking powder. Cream butter;

gradually blend in sugar, beating well after each addition. Add eggs one at a time. Beat well after each. Blend in melted chocolate, vanilla and whole-berry cranberry sauce. Add flour mixture alternately with buttermilk, beating after each addition until smooth. Pour into pan. Bake until cake begins to shrink from sides of pan, about 40 minutes. Cool thoroughly. Ice if desired. Cut into 2 × 2½-inch bars.

■

CHOCOLATE OAT RAISIN BARS

Makes 4 dozen

2 cups sweetened condensed milk
2 ounces (2 squares) unsweetened chocolate
2 cups golden raisins
1 cup butter
1⅓ cups brown sugar, firmly packed

1½ teaspoons vanilla extract
2 cups flour, sifted
¾ teaspoon salt
½ teaspoon baking soda
2½ cups oats (quick cooking)

Preheat oven to 375°. Grease well a 9 × 13 × 2-inch pan. Combine condensed milk and chocolate; heat over boiling water until chocolate melts, stirring occasionally. Remove from heat; stir in raisins and cool slightly. Beat butter, sugar and vanilla together. Sift together flour, salt and baking soda and mix with oats. Add to creamed mixture, mix until crumbly. Press half of mixture into pan. Cover with chocolate-raisin filling; sprinkle with rest of crumbly mixture. Bake until golden brown, about 30 minutes. When cool, cut into 1 × 2-inch bars.

■

CHOCOLATE PETITS FOURS

Elegant, tiny squares covered in a shiny glaze.
Makes 8 dozen

2 cups flour, sifted
⅛ teaspoon salt
½ teaspoon baking powder
1 cup butter
2¼ teaspoons vanilla extract
1 cup brown sugar, firmly packed

10½ ounces (1¾ cups) semisweet chocolate chips
½ cup nuts, very finely chopped
1½ cups powdered sugar, sifted
2 tablespoons light corn syrup
1 tablespoon milk

Preheat oven to 350°. Sift together first three ingredients; set aside. Cream butter, 2 teaspoons vanilla and brown sugar until well mixed. Add flour mixture, blending well. Add chocolate chips and nuts. Spread evenly in a 9 × 12 × 2-inch ungreased pan. Bake until tester inserted in center of cake comes out clean, about 30 minutes. Cool. Combine powdered sugar, corn syrup, milk and remaining vanilla. Spread on cooled cookies. When frosting is set, cut into 1-inch squares.

COCOA CAKE SQUARES

Makes 16

½ *cup butter*
1½ *cups sugar*
2 *eggs*
1 *teaspoon vanilla or almond*
  extract
1 *teaspoon salt*
1 *teaspoon baking powder*

1¾ *cups flour*
½ *cup sour milk*
1 *teaspoon baking soda*
½ *cup cocoa*
½ *cup boiling water*
Frosting (optional)

Preheat oven to 350°. Grease, line with waxed paper and grease again an 8-inch square pan. Cream butter and gradually add sugar, beating until light and fluffy. Beat eggs; add to first mixture with vanilla or almond extract. Beat until fluffy. Sift together salt, baking powder and flour; add about half of this with half the sour milk to the creamed mix. Beat until smooth. Add remaining flour mixture and sour milk; beat again until smooth. Combine baking soda and cocoa; add boiling water, stirring until smooth. Add to batter and stir well. Bake about 30 minutes. Cool in pan 5 minutes, remove. Cool on wire rack. Frost if desired.

SHINY CHOCOLATE SQUARES

Choose a shiny glaze for these rich chocolate squares.
Makes 2 dozen

6 ounces (1 cup) semisweet
　chocolate chips, melted
2 cups flour, sifted
1 teaspoon salt
2½ teaspoons baking powder
⅓ cup cream cheese

¼ cup butter
1 cup sugar
2 eggs
1 cup milk
1 teaspoon vanilla extract
　Glaze of choice

Preheat oven to 350°. Grease and flour a 9 × 13 × 2-inch pan. Melt chocolate over hot, not boiling, water; remove from heat. Sift together flour, salt and baking powder. Blend cream cheese and butter; gradually add sugar. Beat in eggs, one at a time. Stir in melted chocolate. Add flour mixture alternately with milk. Add vanilla. Spread in pan. Bake 35 to 40 minutes. Cool. Top with glaze of choice. Cut into 2-inch squares.

.

FRUIT CHOCOLATE SQUARES

A rich fruit filling makes these very popular.
Makes 36

DOUGH
　½ cup butter
　1 cup sugar
　2 eggs, well beaten
　2 ounces (2 squares) unsweetened
　　chocolate, melted
　2 cups flour
　1 teaspoon baking powder
　½ teaspoon salt
　¼ teaspoon baking soda

¼ cup sour milk
1 teaspoon vanilla extract

FILLING
　¾ cup pineapple, shredded
　½ cup sugar
　2 tablespoons cornstarch
　¼ teaspoon salt
　2 bananas, mashed
　¼ cup lemon juice

For dough, preheat oven to 350°. Grease a baking sheet. Cream butter and sugar thoroughly. Add eggs and melted chocolate, beating well. Mix and sift dry ingredients; add alternately with sour milk to creamed mixture. Add vanilla. Chill dough at least 4 hours. For filling, mix pineapple, sugar and cornstarch; cook until thick. Cool. Add mashed bananas and lemon juice. On a lightly floured board, roll out dough until it is very thin. Cut into 2-inch squares. Put a teaspoon of filling on half of the squares; cover with remaining squares. Crimp edges. Place on baking sheet. Bake 10 to 12 minutes.

NUTTY CHOCOLATE BARS

A multi-layered delight.
Makes 5 dozen

SQUARES

½ teaspoon salt
½ teaspoon baking soda
1¼ cups flour, sifted
½ cup butter, softened
¼ cup sugar
½ cup brown sugar, firmly packed
¼ teaspoon vanilla extract
1 egg
6 ounces (1 cup) semisweet
   chocolate chips

SYRUP

6 ounces (1 cup) semisweet
   chocolate chips
½ cup maple syrup
2 tablespoons butter
¼ teaspoon salt
1 teaspoon vanilla extract
2 cups nuts, finely chopped

For squares, preheat oven to 350°. Sift together first three ingredients. Combine butter, sugars and vanilla; cream well. Beat in egg. Stir in flour mixture and mix well. Spread into ungreased 9 × 13 × 2-inch pan. Bake 15 minutes, remove from oven and sprinkle with chocolate chips. Let melt. For syrup, combine 1 cup chocolate chips, maple syrup, butter, salt, vanilla and nuts. Spread evenly over squares and return to oven 8 minutes. Cool; cut into 1 × 1½-inch bars.

OLD-FASHIONED CHOCOLATE SQUARES

Flourless, rich and light.
Makes 4½ dozen

1 cup brown sugar, firmly packed
4 eggs, separated
1 cup crushed ginger snaps
1 cup ground almonds
1 teaspoon baking powder
½ teaspoon cinnamon

½ teaspoon ground cloves
8 ounces sweet chocolate, grated
1 tablespoon wine
   Icing (optional)

Preheat oven to 350°. Grease and flour well a 9 × 13-inch pan. Beat brown sugar with egg yolks, ginger snaps, ground almonds, baking powder, cinnamon, cloves, grated chocolate and wine. Beat egg whites; add to mixture. Place in pan. Bake until tester inserted in center comes out clean. Cool in pan. Ice if desired; cut into 1½-inch squares.

UPSIDE DOWN
CHOCOLATE CAKE SQUARES

Makes 16

½ cup nuts, chopped
6 ounces (1 cup) semisweet
  chocolate chips, melted
1 cup powdered sugar, sifted
⅓ cup evaporated milk
1 cup plus 2 tablespoons flour,
  sifted

½ teaspoon salt
1½ teaspoons baking powder
¾ cup sugar
¼ cup butter, softened
1 egg
½ cup milk
1 teaspoon vanilla extract

Preheat oven to 350°. Line an 8-inch square pan with waxed paper. Sprinkle nuts into pan. Melt chocolate over hot, not boiling, water. Add powdered sugar and evaporated milk; beat until smooth. Spread this mixture over nuts. Sift together flour, salt and baking powder. Mix sugar and butter, beating until blended. Beat in egg. Stir in flour mixture alternately with milk. When well mixed, add vanilla. Pour into pan over chocolate mixture. Bake until tester inserted in center of cake comes out clean, about 45 minutes. Cool in pan 5 minutes; invert on wire rack. Peel off waxed paper. Cool. Cut into 2-inch squares.

·

SWEET CHOCOLATE CAKE SQUARES

Buttermilk adds a delicate touch to these.
Makes about 3 dozen

4 ounces sweet chocolate
1½ cups flour, sifted
1 cup sugar
½ teaspoon baking soda
½ teaspoon baking powder
½ teaspoon salt
⅓ cup butter

¾ cup buttermilk
1 teaspoon vanilla or almond
  extract
2 eggs
Frosting of choice

Preheat oven to 350°. Line bottom of 9-inch square pan with waxed paper. Melt chocolate over low heat; cool. Sift together dry ingredients. Stir butter to soften; add flour mixture, half the buttermilk and vanilla or almond extract. Mix to dampen flour; beat 3 or 4 minutes at medium speed of electric mixer, scraping bowl occasionally. Add melted chocolate, eggs and remaining buttermilk; beat another minute. Pour batter into pan. Bake until tester inserted in center comes out clean. Cool in pan 15 minutes; turn out. Completely cool on wire rack. Cut into 1½-inch squares; spread with frosting of choice.

CHOCOLATE TOFFEE BITES

Old-fashioned bites with crunchy toffee layers.
Makes 16

1½ ounces (1½ squares) unsweetened
  chocolate
16 wafers, vanilla or chocolate
1 cup nuts, finely chopped
¼ pound butter
1 cup powdered sugar

3 eggs, separated
1 teaspoon vanilla extract
  Whipping cream, whipped
  (optional)

Grease a 9-inch square pan. Melt chocolate in top of double boiler over hot, not boiling, water. Leave over hot water; set aside. Roll wafers to crumbs and combine with nuts. Cream butter with powdered sugar until fluffy and light; beat in egg yolks until batter is thick. Add melted chocolate and vanilla. Blend. Beat egg whites until they form stiff peaks; fold into chocolate mixture. Place half the crumb mix in pan; pour batter over slowly and evenly. Top with remaining crumbs. Cover with waxed paper. Chill at least 24 hours. Cut into 2-inch squares before serving. Top each with whipped cream if desired.

TOFFEE CHOCOLATE BARS

Makes about 3 dozen

2¼ cups flour, sifted
¼ teaspoon salt
½ teaspoon baking powder
1 cup butter
1 cup brown sugar, firmly packed

1 teaspoon instant coffee
1 teaspoon almond extract
6 ounces (1 cup) semisweet
  chocolate chips
½ cup pecans, finely chopped

Preheat oven to 350°. Grease a 10 × 15 × 1-inch pan. Sift together dry ingredients. Blend butter, brown sugar, instant coffee and almond extract. Blend in dry ingredients slowly. Stir in chocolate chips and nuts. Place in pan. Bake until tester inserted in center of cake comes out clean, 20 to 25 minutes. While still warm, cut into 2-inch squares.

CHOCOLATE DREAM BARS

Chopped dates make these bars special.
Makes about 2 dozen

1¼ cups sweetened condensed milk
2 cups graham cracker crumbs
6 ounces (1 cup) semisweet
   chocolate chips

1 teaspoon vanilla extract
½ teaspoon salt
1¼ cup dates, finely chopped

Preheat oven to 350°. Grease an 8-inch square pan. Mix all ingredients until completely blended. Place batter in pan. Bake about 30 minutes. Cool. Cut into 1½-inch squares.

BLACK WALNUT BROWNIES

Makes 16

½ cup butter
1 cup sugar
2 eggs, well beaten
2 ounces (2 squares) unsweetened
   chocolate, melted

1 teaspoon black walnut flavoring
⅔ cup flour
¼ teaspoon baking powder
¼ teaspoon salt
1 cup nuts, finely chopped

Preheat oven to 350°. Grease an 8-inch square pan. Cream butter; gradually add sugar, continuing to beat until fluffy. Add eggs, melted chocolate and black walnut flavoring. Beat well. Sift together dry ingredients; add to mixture. Beat until batter is smooth. Stir in nuts. Bake about 30 minutes. Immediately cut into 2-inch squares.

APPLESAUCE BROWNIES

A heavenly combination of chocolate and applesauce.
Makes about 2 dozen

2 ounces (2 squares) unsweetened
   chocolate
½ cup butter
½ cup applesauce
2 eggs, well beaten
1 cup sugar
1 teaspoon vanilla extract

½ teaspoon almond extract
¼ teaspoon salt
½ teaspoon baking soda
½ teaspoon baking powder
1 cup flour, sifted
1 cup nuts, finely chopped

Preheat oven to 350°. Grease and flour a 9-inch square pan. Melt chocolate and butter over hot water. Add applesauce, eggs, sugar and vanilla and almond extracts; blend well. Sift together dry ingredients; blend into first mixture. Add nuts. Spread batter in pan. Bake until tester inserted in center of pan comes out clean, 35 to 40 minutes. While still hot, cut into 1¾-inch bars.

FUDGE COOKIES

Makes 16

2 eggs, beaten	¹⁄₁₆ teaspoon salt
1 cup sugar	2 tablespoons cocoa
½ cup butter	1 cup nuts, finely chopped
1 teaspoon vanilla extract	
¾ cup flour	Powdered sugar

Preheat oven to 300°. Grease an 8-inch square pan. Combine first 8 ingredients. Mix well. Place in pan. Bake about 25 minutes. Cool in pan 15 minutes, then cut into 2-inch squares. Roll in powdered sugar.

MARY'S CHOCOLATE SQUARES

Basic and simply wonderful.
Makes about 2 dozen

1 cup plus 2 tablespoons flour, sifted	½ cup sugar
½ teaspoon salt	1 teaspoon vanilla extract
½ teaspoon baking soda	1 egg
½ cup butter, softened	½ cup nuts, chopped
½ cup brown sugar, firmly packed	6 ounces (1 cup) semisweet chocolate chips

Preheat oven to 375°. Grease a 9 × 13 × 2-inch pan. Sift together first three ingredients. Blend butter, brown sugar, sugar and vanilla; beat in egg. Add flour mixture and mix well. Stir in nuts. Spread in pan. Sprinkle chocolate chips over top of batter. Place in oven a minute, then remove. Run a knife through batter to marbleize. Return to oven and complete baking, 10 to 12 minutes more. Cool. Cut into 2-inch squares.

BROWNIE BRAN BARS

Bran adds body to these rich bars.
Makes 16

1 cup sugar
1 cup butter
2 eggs, beaten
2 ounces (2 squares) unsweetened
    chocolate, melted

⅓ cup flour
½ teaspoon salt
½ cup bran
1 cup nuts, finely chopped
1 teaspoon vanilla extract

Preheat oven to 350°. Grease an 8 × 8 × 2-inch pan. Cream sugar and butter; beating in eggs. Melt chocolate over hot water; add to butter mixture and beat thoroughly. Mix flour, salt, bran and nuts together; add to mixture. Add vanilla and mix well. Spread in pan. Bake about 45 minutes. Cool about 10 minutes; cut into 2-inch bars.

BROWNIE CHEESE SQUARES

Cottage cheese is the magic ingredient here.
Makes 2 dozen

1¼ cups sugar
½ cup plus 2 tablespoons butter
3 eggs
2 ounces (2 squares) unsweetened
    chocolate, melted
1 teaspoon vanilla or almond
    extract

1 cup flour
½ teaspoon salt
1 cup nuts, finely chopped
1 cup cottage cheese
1 tablespoon cornstarch

Preheat oven to 375°. Grease well an 8-inch square pan. Cream 1 cup sugar and all but 2 tablespoons butter until light and fluffy. Add 2 eggs, chocolate and ½ teaspoon vanilla or almond extract. Blend thoroughly. Sift together flour and salt; blend into creamed mixture. Stir in nuts (batter will be fairly stiff). For cheese mixture, combine remaining sugar, butter, egg and vanilla or almond extract with cottage cheese and cornstarch. Beat until thoroughly blended (mixture will be thin). Spread half the chocolate batter in pan. Pour cheese mixture over batter. Drop remaining chocolate batter by spoonfuls over the cheese mixture. Carefully swirl batter into cheese mixture to marble. Bake until tester inserted in center comes out clean and surface is shiny, about 45 minutes. While still warm, cut into 1½-inch squares.

BLONDE BROWNIES

Great tasting and great looking.
Makes 2 dozen

½ teaspoon salt
⅛ teaspoon baking soda
½ teaspoon baking powder
1 cup flour, sifted
½ cup nuts, chopped
⅓ cup unsalted butter

1 cup brown sugar, firmly packed
1 egg
1 teaspoon vanilla extract
½ teaspoon black walnut flavoring
1½ ounces (¼ cup) semisweet
   chocolate chips

Preheat oven to 350°. Grease a 9-inch square pan. Sift together dry ingredients. Add nuts, mixing well. Melt butter in small pan, remove from heat and add brown sugar. Blend carefully. Add dry ingredients a little at a time, mixing well after each addition. Add egg and vanilla; blend well. Place in pan. Sprinkle chocolate chips over top. Bake until cake tester inserted in center of cake comes out clean, 20 to 25 minutes. Cut into bars.

CHOCOLATE CHIP SQUARES

Makes 1½ dozen

½ cup flour, sifted
½ teaspoon baking powder
¼ teaspoon salt
½ cup sugar
1 egg, beaten well

1 teaspoon butter, melted
2 teaspoons hot water
1 cup nuts, finely chopped
6 ounces (1 cup) semisweet
   chocolate chips

Preheat oven to 325°. Grease, line with waxed paper and grease again an 8 × 8 × 2-inch pan. Sift flour, baking powder and salt together three times. Gradually add sugar to egg; beat thoroughly. Add butter and water, then nuts and chocolate chips, mixing thoroughly. Add flour mixture, blending well. Pour into pan. Bake until tester inserted in center of pan comes out clean, 25 to 30 minutes. Remove from pan. Cut into 2¼-inch squares.

YUMMY CHOCOLATE BARS

Chewy bars full of chopped nuts and oatmeal.
Makes 16

½ cup plus 1 tablespoon butter,
  softened
½ cup brown sugar, firmly packed
1 teaspoon vanilla extract
1 egg

½ cup sifted flour
½ cup rolled oats
6 ounces (1 cup) semisweet
  chocolate chips
½ cup nuts, chopped

Preheat oven to 350°. Grease a 7 × 11 × 1½-inch pan. Beat ½ cup butter, brown sugar and vanilla until creamy. Beat in egg. Add flour and oats. Place in pan. Bake about 20 minutes. Cool. Melt chocolate chips and remaining butter over hot, not boiling, water. Spread over top and sprinkle with nuts. Cut into 1¼ × 3½-inch bars.

•

BROWNIE-MOCHA-WINE SQUARES

These are especially good cold.
Makes 3 dozen

¼ cup sherry
1 teaspoon instant coffee
¼ teaspoon cinnamon
¼ teaspoon allspice

2 eggs
1 (21.5 ounces) package fudge
  brownie mix
1 cup nuts, chopped

Preheat oven to 350°. Grease an 8-inch square pan. Mix all ingredients except nuts until well blended; add nuts. Place in pan. Bake until tester inserted in center of pan comes out clean, about 25 minutes. Cool. Cut into 1½-inch squares.

•

FUDGE BROWNIES DIVINE

Fudgy and rich—truly divine.
Makes 2 dozen

4 ounces (4 squares) unsweetened
  chocolate
½ cup butter
4 eggs
2 cups sugar

1 cup flour, sifted
1 teaspoon vanilla extract
½ teaspoon black walnut flavoring
1 cup nuts, chopped

Preheat oven to 325°. Grease a 9 × 9 × 2-inch pan. Melt chocolate and butter together over hot water; cool slightly. Beat eggs until foamy. Gradually add sugar, 2 tablespoons at a time. Beat thoroughly after each addition. Blend in chocolate mixture, then stir in flour. Add vanilla, black walnut flavoring and nuts. Place in pan. Bake until tester inserted in center comes out clean, about 45 minutes. Cool in pan. Cut into 1½ × 2-inch bars.

■

HONEY NUT BROWNIES

Honey provides its distinct sweetness to these.
Makes 16

2 ounces (2 squares) semisweet
   chocolate, melted
1¼ cups unsalted butter
½ cup sugar
½ cup honey
2 eggs, beaten

1 cup nuts, finely chopped
¼ teaspoon baking soda
¼ teaspoon baking powder
½ cup flour
1 teaspoon vanilla extract

Preheat oven to 300°. Grease an 8-inch square pan, and line with waxed paper. Melt chocolate with butter. Add sugar, honey and beaten eggs. Blend well. Add nuts to dry ingredients which have been sifted together; add to chocolate mixture and stir until well blended. Place in pan. Bake until tester inserted in center comes out clean, about 45 minutes. Cut into 2-inch bars.

■

UNBAKED BROWNIES

Makes 2 dozen

2 ounces (2 squares) semisweet
   chocolate
1⅓ cups sweetened condensed milk

2 cups crushed vanilla wafers
1 cup nuts, finely chopped

Grease well an 8-inch square pan. Melt chocolate in double boiler. Add condensed milk. Cook 5 minutes, stirring constantly until mixture thickens. Add vanilla wafer crumbs and ½ cup nuts. Sprinkle ¼ cup nuts in pan. Spread chocolate mixture over nuts in pan; sprinkle remaining nuts on top. Refrigerate overnight. Cut into squares.

■

WESTERN BROWNIES

Makes 16

2 cups crushed graham crackers,
  firmly packed
4 ounces (⅔ cup) semisweet
  chocolate chips

½ cup nuts, chopped
1¾ cups sweetened condensed milk

Preheat oven to 350°. Grease, line with waxed paper and grease again an 8 × 8 × 2-inch square pan. Mix crushed graham crackers, chocolate chips and nuts. Blend in condensed milk. Spread into pan. Bake until top is golden brown, about 35 minutes. Remove from oven. Cool in pan about 10 minutes. Remove from pan; peel off waxed paper. Cut into 2-inch squares; cool completely.

LIGHT AND DARK BROWNIES

Two-layered and two-toned.
Makes 1½ dozen

1 cup brown sugar, firmly packed
¼ cup butter, softened
1½ cups flour, sifted
¼ teaspoon baking powder
¼ teaspoon salt
½ cup sugar
⅓ cup vegetable shortening

2 tablespoons water
6 ounces (1 cup) semisweet
  chocolate chips
1 teaspoon vanilla extract
2 eggs
½ cup nuts, chopped

Preheat oven to 350°. Grease a 9-inch square pan. Combine brown sugar and butter; beat until creamy. Sift half the flour with half the baking powder; gradually blend into brown sugar mixture. Press this dough into pan. Bake 10 minutes. Sift remaining flour and baking powder with salt. Combine sugar, vegetable shortening and water in a saucepan. Bring just to a boil, stirring constantly. Remove from heat. Add chocolate and vanilla; blend well. Add eggs, one at a time, beating well. Stir in flour mixture and nuts. Spread over partially baked cookie layer. Return to oven; bake another 20 minutes. Cool about 10 minutes. Cut into 1½ × 3-inch pieces.

MARSHMALLOW BROWNIES

Topped with a creamy layer of melted marshmallows and chocolate.
Makes 2 dozen

1 cup flour, sifted
½ teaspoon salt
½ teaspoon baking soda
12 ounces (2 cups) semisweet chocolate chips
¾ cup sugar

½ cup butter, softened
2 eggs
1 teaspoon vanilla extract
1 cup nuts, chopped
2 cups miniature marshmallows

Preheat oven to 350°. Grease a 9-inch square pan. Sift together flour, salt and soda; set aside. Melt 1 cup chocolate chips over hot, but not boiling, water; remove from heat. Cream sugar, ½ cup butter and eggs; blend in melted chocolate. Stir in flour mixture. Add vanilla and nuts. Spread in pan. Bake until tester inserted in center of pan comes out clean, 35 to 40 minutes. Remove from oven. Immediately place marshmallows on top of cake. Melt remaining cup of chocolate chips and 1 tablespoon butter over hot water; pour slowly over marshmallows. Cool; cut into 1¾-inch squares.

COFFEE BROWNIES

Makes 3 dozen

1½ cups flour, sifted
1 teaspoon salt
1 teaspoon baking powder
⅔ cup butter
3 ounces (3 squares) unsweetened chocolate

3 tablespoons instant coffee
4 eggs
2 cups sugar
1 cup nuts, chopped
1 teaspoon black walnut flavoring

Preheat oven to 350°. Grease and flour a 9 × 13 × 2-inch pan. Sift first three ingredients together. Melt chocolate and butter over hot water; blend in coffee. Beat together eggs and sugar, until sugar is no longer grainy. Add chocolate mixture to eggs, then flour mixture. Mix well. Stir in black walnut flavoring and nuts. Place batter in pan. Bake until tester inserted in center of a brownie comes out clean, 25 to 30 minutes. Cool in pan. Cut into 1½ × 2-inch bars.

MARBLEIZED BROWNIES

Appealing to the eye as well as the palate.
Makes 21

2 eggs, separated
1 cup sugar
½ cup butter, melted
½ cup nuts, finely chopped

¾ cup flour, sifted
2 tablespoons whipping cream
1 ounce (1 square) unsweetened
  chocolate, melted

Preheat oven to 350°. Grease, line with waxed paper and grease again a 9-inch square pan. Beat egg whites until stiff. Add about ½ the sugar and beat until well blended. Add remaining sugar to egg yolks and beat until thick and lemon colored; add butter and nuts. Stir in flour and whipping cream; fold in beaten whites. Place ½ of the batter by teaspoonfuls in pan, leaving spaces between. Add chocolate to remaining batter and place by teaspoonfuls into spaces left in pan; stir a little with a fork to blend. Bake about 30 minutes. Cool in pan until lukewarm; lift out by waxed paper. Peel off waxed paper. Cut into 1½ × 2½-inch bars.

COCONUT BROWNIES DIVINE

Coconut makes these moist and chewy.
Makes about 2 dozen

4 ounces (4 squares) unsweetened
  chocolate
½ cup butter
4 eggs
2 cups sugar

1 cup flour, sifted
1 teaspoon vanilla extract
½ teaspoon almond extract
¾ cup shredded coconut

Preheat oven to 325°. Grease a 9 × 9 × 2-inch pan. Melt chocolate and butter together over hot water; cool slightly. Beat eggs until foamy. Gradually add sugar, 2 tablespoons at a time, beating thoroughly after each addition. Blend in chocolate mixture, then stir in flour. Add vanilla and almond extracts and coconut. Place in pan. Bake until tester inserted in center comes out clean, about 45 minutes. Cool in pan, then cut into 1¾-inch bars.

RIPPLED BROWNIES

Crowned with an almond-flavored cheese layer.
Makes 32

2 cups flour, sifted
1 teaspoon baking powder
½ teaspoon salt
8 ounces sweet chocolate
1 cup cream cheese, softened

2 cups sugar
4 eggs
½ teaspoon almond extract
2 teaspoons vanilla extract
1 cup nuts, chopped

Preheat oven to 350°. Grease two 8-inch square pans. Sift together flour, baking powder and salt. Melt chocolate over low heat. Set aside; cool. Cream softened cheese. Gradually add sugar, creaming until light and fluffy. Blend in eggs. Add flour mixture and almond extract. Set 1 cup of batter aside. Blend chocolate, vanilla and nuts into remaining batter. Spread about 1 cup of chocolate batter in each pan. Spoon measured cheese batter over top, spreading carefully with spatula to cover chocolate batter. Spread remaining chocolate batter evenly over cheese batter in each pan. Bake until tops spring back when pressed lightly in center, about 30 minutes. Cool. Cut into 2-inch squares.

·

BROWNIE TWINKLES

Makes 5½ dozen

1 (21.5 ounces) package brownie
   mix
2 eggs
⅓ cup cooking oil

½ cup nuts, very finely chopped
   Powdered sugar

Preheat oven to 350°. Grease baking sheet. Mix first four ingredients together; chill about 4 hours. Sprinkle powdered sugar on waxed paper. Drop dough by teaspoonfuls into powdered sugar; roll and shape into 1-inch balls, coating completely. Place about 2 inches apart on baking sheet. Bake 10 minutes, being careful not to overbake.

·

Drop Cookies

❖

ALMOND CHOCOLATE COOKIES

Delicate, iced cookies.
Makes about 35

1 cup sugar	½ teaspoon ground cloves
6 eggs, separated	½ teaspoon allspice
⅛ teaspoon salt	½ lemon peel, grated
8 ounces sweet chocolate, grated	2 teaspoons lemon juice
1 cup almonds, ground	½ cup flour or more as needed
1 teaspoon cinnamon	2 cups powdered sugar, sifted

Preheat oven to 375°. Beat sugar and egg yolks. Beat 3 egg whites, adding ¹⁄₁₆ teaspoon salt. Stir in grated chocolate, almonds, spices, lemon peel and 1 teaspoon lemon juice. Add egg yolk mixture; blend well. Add enough flour to make a stiff dough. Press into a 10 × 15 × 1-inch jelly-roll pan or roll out thin. To make icing, beat 3 egg whites until stiff, adding powdered sugar, remaining 1 teaspoon lemon juice and ¹⁄₁₆ teaspoon salt. Mix all ingredients together, beating well. Spread on dough. Bake until icing is lightly browned, about 20 minutes. Remove from oven; cut into 2-inch squares while hot. When cool, remove from pan with a spatula.

∎

CHOCOLATE SPRITZ COOKIES

Makes 3 dozen

½ cup butter	1 egg
¼ cup sugar	½ teaspoon vanilla extract
1½ ounces (1½ squares) unsweetened chocolate, melted	½ teaspoon almond extract
	1¼ cups flour
1 tablespoon whipping cream	½ teaspoon baking powder

Preheat oven to 400°. Cream butter and sugar; add melted chocolate and whipping cream. Beat egg and add vanilla and almond extracts. Sift together dry ingredients and add, mixing well. Wrap in waxed paper and chill until firm. Roll dough out on a lightly floured board to about ¼-inch thickness. Cut with cookie cutter into 2-inch circles. Bake on greased baking sheets until lightly browned, about 8 minutes. Cool in pan 1 minute; complete cooling on wire rack.

STORING COOKIES

- *To keep cookies crisp, place them in a container with a loose fitting cover.*
- *To keep cookies soft, use a tight fitting cover on the container.*
- *Place either a slice of bread or about ¼ apple in the container to help keep soft cookies fresh. Change bread or apple as it dries out.*
- *To protect fragile cookies, store them in single layers separated by sheets of waxed paper.*

CHOCOLATE APRICOT COOKIES

Makes about 3 dozen

½ cup butter
1 cup sugar
1 egg, beaten
1 ounce (1 square) unsweetened chocolate, melted
1½ cups flour

1 teaspoon baking powder
½ teaspoon salt
⅓ cup milk
1 cup dried apricots, finely chopped
1 teaspoon vanilla extract

Preheat oven to 375°. Grease a baking sheet. Cream butter and sugar thoroughly; add beaten egg and melted chocolate. Mix and sift dry ingredients. Stir in apricots. Add alternately with milk to creamed mixture. Add vanilla. Drop by teaspoonfuls onto baking sheet. Bake until lightly browned, about 12 minutes.

CHOCOLATE NIBBLES

Makes 6 dozen

½ cup butter
1 cup sugar
3 ounces (3 squares) unsweetened chocolate
2 eggs

1 teaspoon vanilla extract
2¼ cups flour
1 teaspoon baking soda
½ teaspoon salt

Preheat oven to 375°. Grease a baking sheet well. Cream butter and sugar. Melt chocolate over hot water; add to first mixture. Beat eggs; add to chocolate mixture. Add vanilla. Sift together dry ingredients and add, mixing well. Wrap in waxed paper; chill until firm. Roll on a lightly floured board to about ⅛-inch thickness; cut into 1 × 3-inch bites. Place on baking sheet. Bake 10 minutes. Cool in pan 1 minute; complete cooling on wire rack.

CHOCOLATE BUTTER COOKIES

Quick cookies with a gourmet touch.
Makes about 3 dozen

1 (20 ounces) package refrigerated
   slice-and-bake sugar cookies
1½ cups powdered sugar
1 tablespoon arrowroot
¾ cup cream cheese, softened

½ cup nuts, chopped
½ teaspoon rum flavoring
4½ ounces (¾ cup) semisweet
   chocolate chips
¼ cup butter

Preheat oven to 375°. Slice cookie dough into 1-inch thick slices; cut each into fourths. Place on ungreased baking sheet. Bake until golden on top, 9 to 13 minutes. Remove from oven; indent each center with thumb. Mix powdered sugar, arrowroot and cream cheese in a small bowl until smooth; stir in rum flavoring and nuts. Drop into indentations on baked cookies. Allow to set. Make topping by melting chocolate chips and butter over low heat. Spoon this over cream cheese filling and cookies.

CHOCOLATE MACAROONS

Makes about 2 dozen

2 cups almonds, ground
8 ounces sweet chocolate, grated
2 cups powdered sugar, sifted

2 level teaspoons cornstarch
8 egg whites, beaten

Preheat oven to 375°. Mix all ingredients well. Dampen hands, then drop by teaspoonfuls onto hand. Roll into balls and drop on baking sheet. Bake until very slight crust forms, 15 to 20 minutes. Cool completely before removing from pan.

CHOCOLATE LADIES MACAROONS

Light, crisp and chewy.
Makes 1½ dozen

2 egg whites
1 cup sugar
⅛ teaspoon salt
½ teaspoon vanilla extract

1½ cups coconut, shredded
1½ ounces (1½ squares) unsweetened
   chocolate, melted

Preheat oven to 275°. Grease a cookie sheet. Beat egg whites until stiff; gradually beat in sugar and salt. After all sugar is added, beat well. Add vanilla. Fold in coconut and chocolate, which has been melted over hot water. Drop by teaspoonfuls onto cookie sheet. Turn off oven. Let stand in warm oven 1 hour.

CHOCOLATE COCONUT COOKIES

Buttery and moist.
Makes 3½ dozen

½ cup butter
½ cup sugar
½ cup brown sugar, firmly packed
1 egg, beaten
1½ cups flour
½ teaspoon baking soda

¼ teaspoon salt
4½ ounces (¾ cup) semisweet chocolate chips
½ cup coconut, shredded (moist pack)

Preheat oven to 375°. Grease a baking sheet. Cream butter, brown sugar and sugar; add beaten egg. Sift together dry ingredients; add to creamed mixture. Chop chocolate chips and add to mixture with coconut. Mix well. Drop by teaspoonfuls on baking sheet. Bake until lightly browned, about 10 minutes.

CHOCOLATE COCONUT MACAROONS

Makes about 2½ dozen

1 cup almond paste
1 cup sugar
3 egg whites
2 ounces (2 squares) unsweetened chocolate, melted

1 cup coconut, shredded
¼ teaspoon salt
½ teaspoon vanilla extract
30 candied cherries

Preheat oven to 300°. Line baking sheet with waxed paper. Rub almond paste with back of spoon until smooth. Add sugar and continue to work until well blended. Add egg whites one at a time, beating well after each addition. Blend in melted chocolate, coconut, salt and vanilla. Drop mixture by tablespoonfuls onto baking sheet to form macaroon shapes. Moisten tops by shaking damp cloth over them. Bake until very lightly browned, about 30 minutes. While still warm, press a candied cherry into center of each.

CHOCOLATE
BRAZIL NUT COOKIES

Makes 4 dozen

8 ounces sweet chocolate
2 cups flour, sifted
½ teaspoon salt
½ teaspoon baking soda
¾ cup butter
¾ cup sugar

2 eggs
½ teaspoon vanilla extract
½ teaspoon black walnut flavoring
¾ cup Brazil nuts, chopped
Icing (optional)

Preheat oven to 350°. Grease a cookie sheet. Melt chocolate over hot water; cool. Sift together flour, soda and salt. Cream butter and sugar together until light and fluffy. Add eggs, beating well. Add melted chocolate; blend well. Add flour and blend again. Add vanilla, black walnut flavoring and nuts. Drop by teaspoonfuls onto cookie sheet. Bake until done, about 10 minutes. Spread with icing if desired.

·

CHOCOLATE KISSES

Makes 2 dozen

4 egg whites
¾ cup sugar

½ cup flour
4 ounces sweet chocolate, grated

Preheat oven to 250°. Cover baking sheet with brown paper. Beat egg whites until stiff enough to form peaks, but not dry. Add ½ the sugar, a tablespoon at a time, beating after each addition. Combine remaining sugar with flour. Carefully fold into egg whites. Add grated chocolate. Drop by teaspoonfuls onto baking sheet. Bake until very lightly browned, about 50 minutes.

·

CHOCOLATE NUT CRISPS

Makes 4 dozen

1 cup butter
2 cups powdered sugar, sifted
2 egg yolks
1 teaspoon almond extract
½ teaspoon vanilla extract

2 cups flour, sifted
¼ teaspoon salt
1 cup nuts, diced and roasted
4½ ounces (¾ cup) semisweet
  chocolate chips

Preheat oven to 375°. Grease a cookie sheet. Blend butter and ½ the sugar; beat until fluffy. Add egg yolks and vanilla and almond extracts; beat in well. Add flour, salt, nuts and chocolate chips; stir until well mixed. Drop onto cookie sheet by teaspoonfuls. Bake until lightly browned, 10 to 12 minutes. While cookies are still warm, dust with remaining powdered sugar.

CHOCOLATE OATMEAL COOKIES

A chocolate version of the ever popular oatmeal cookie.
Makes 3½ dozen

8 ounces sweet chocolate	½ cup butter
¾ cup flour, sifted	½ cup sugar
½ teaspoon salt	½ cup brown sugar, firmly packed
½ teaspoon baking soda	1 egg
½ cup nuts, chopped	½ teaspoon vanilla extract
1 cup oatmeal	½ teaspoon almond extract

Preheat oven to 375°. Cut each square of chocolate into small pieces. Sift flour, measure and then add baking soda and salt; resift. Add chocolate, nuts and oatmeal. Cream butter; gradually add both sugars, creaming until light and fluffy. Add egg and vanilla and almond extracts; beat thoroughly. Add flour mixture; blend completely. Drop about 2 inches apart onto an ungreased cookie sheet by teaspoonfuls. Bake until browned, about 12 minutes.

CHOCOLATE FLYING SAUCERS

Makes 3 dozen

¼ cup shortening	¼ teaspoon vanilla extract
¼ cup butter	1 cup flour, sifted
1 ounce (1 square) unsweetened chocolate	¼ teaspoon salt
	¾ cup nuts, finely chopped
½ cup sugar	4 ounces (⅔ cup) semisweet chocolate chips
1 egg, separated	

Preheat oven to 350°. Melt chocolate over hot, not boiling, water. Cool slightly. Cream shortening and butter together; add melted chocolate. Add sugar, egg yolk and vanilla; mix thoroughly. Sift flour and salt together; stir into mixture. Beat egg white slightly with fork. Roll dough into balls, allowing about 1 teaspoon per ball. Dip balls in egg white and roll in nuts. Place an inch apart on an ungreased cookie sheet. Press thumb gently into center of each. Bake until set, 10 to 12 minutes. Transfer to wire rack. Place 3 or 4 chocolate chips in each indentation. When chocolate chips have melted (it will take just a few minutes), spread evenly over cookie.

CHOCOLATE COOKIES

Makes 2 dozen

1½ cups flour
½ cup sweetened cocoa mix
1 teaspoon salt
½ teaspoon baking soda

½ cup butter
½ cup molasses
1 tablespoon white vinegar
Frosting of choice

Preheat oven to 350°. Sift first four ingredients together. Cut in butter with pastry blender until mixture resembles large peas. Mix molasses and vinegar into mixture; blend well. Chill several hours in refrigerator. Roll out on well-floured board to about ⅛-inch thickness. Cut with cookie cutter. Bake on ungreased cookie sheet. Let stand about 1 minute before removing from cookie sheet. Coat with frosting of choice.

CHOCOLATE CRISP COOKIES

Makes about 7 dozen

½ cup butter
1 cup sugar
1 egg, beaten
2 ounces (2 squares) unsweetened
   chocolate, melted

2½ cups flour
½ teaspoon salt
½ teaspoon baking soda
½ teaspoon allspice
2 tablespoons milk

Preheat oven to 350°. Thoroughly cream butter with sugar. Add beaten egg and melted chocolate. Mix and sift dry ingredients. Add alternately with milk to creamed mixture. Chill dough, then roll on slightly floured board to ⅛-inch thickness. Cut into desired shapes and place on greased baking sheet. Bake until lightly browned, 5 to 7 minutes.

CHOCOLATE CREAM DROPS

Easy, dark and delicious.
Makes about 4 dozen

¼ cup butter
¾ cup sugar
1 egg
½ cup sour cream
½ teaspoon vanilla extract
½ teaspoon butter flavoring
1⅜ cups flour

¼ teaspoon baking powder
¼ teaspoon baking soda
¼ teaspoon salt
1 ounce (1 square) unsweetened
  chocolate, melted
Icing

Preheat oven to 425°. Lightly grease a cookie sheet. Mix butter, sugar and egg. Stir in sour cream, vanilla and butter flavoring. Sift together dry ingredients; add to first mixture. Fold in melted chocolate. Chill 1 hour in refrigerator. Drop by rounded teaspoonfuls about 2 inches apart on cookie sheet. Bake until delicately browned, 8 to 10 minutes. Ice with desired icing.

■

CHOCOLATE DROPS

Makes 5 dozen

½ cup butter, softened
1¼ cups sugar
2 eggs
2 ounces (2 squares) unsweetened
  chocolate, melted
¼ cup milk
1½ teaspoons vanilla extract

2 cups flour, sifted
½ teaspoon salt
½ teaspoon baking soda
½ teaspoon baking powder
½ cup nuts, finely chopped
¾ cup oatmeal
Chocolate frosting of choice

Preheat oven to 350°. Cream butter and sugar until fluffy. Add eggs, melted chocolate, milk and vanilla. Mix well. Sift together dry ingredients; add to cream mixture, blending well. Stir in nuts and oatmeal. Place dough in refrigerator about 2 hours. Drop by teaspoonfuls onto an ungreased cookie sheet, leaving 2 to 3 inches between cookies. Bake until lightly browned, 10 to 12 minutes. Cool on wire rack. Spread with chocolate frosting of choice.

■

CHOCOLATE NUT COOKIES

Makes about 2½ dozen

1 cup butter, softened
1 (14.5 ounces) package chocolate
    frosting mix
2 teaspoons almond or vanilla
    extract
1 cup chopped candied mixed fruit
    or ½ cup raisins

1½ cups flour
¼ teaspoon salt
    Fudge frosting, about 1 cup
1 cup pecan halves

Preheat oven to 300°. Mix butter, frosting mix and vanilla or almond extract. Add flour, candied fruit and salt; mix well. Shape into small balls. Place 2 inches apart on ungreased cookie sheet; flatten. Place 1 teaspoon frosting on each cookie and top with a nut. Bake about 15 minutes.

CHOCOLATE TURTLE COOKIES

Fanciful and fun to make.
Makes 24 to 30

1½ cups flour, sifted
¼ teaspoon salt
½ teaspoon baking soda
½ cup plus 1 tablespoon butter
½ cup brown sugar, firmly packed
2 eggs, separated
¼ teaspoon vanilla extract

⅛ teaspoon almond extract
⅛ teaspoon maple flavoring
1 cup pecan halves
2 ounces (2 squares) unsweetened
    chocolate
¼ cup milk
1 cup powdered sugar, sifted

Preheat oven to 350°. Grease a baking sheet. Sift dry ingredients together. Cream all but 1 tablespoon butter and brown sugar together. Add 1 egg and 1 yolk; beat well. Blend in vanilla and almond extracts and maple flavoring. Gradually add dry ingredients, mixing thoroughly. Chill dough. Arrange pecan halves in groups of 5 on greased baking sheet to resemble the head and legs of turtles. Mold rounded teaspoonfuls of dough into balls, dip bottom into unbeaten whites and press lightly onto the nuts. Make sure tips of nuts will show when baked. Bake until done, 10 to 12 minutes. Cool. Make frosting by combining chocolate, milk and remaining butter in top of double boiler. Heat over boiling water until chocolate melts; blend until smooth. Remove from heat. Add powdered sugar, beating until smooth and glossy. Add more powdered sugar if too thin. Coat Turtles.

CHOCOLATE ORANGE CHIP COOKIES

Makes 4 dozen

6 ounces (1 cup) semisweet
   chocolate chips, melted
½ cup butter
1½ cups sugar
2 eggs
2 cups flour, sifted

½ teaspoon salt
1 teaspoon baking soda
⅓ cup frozen orange juice
   concentrate, thawed
1 tablespoon orange peel, grated

Preheat oven to 350°. Grease a baking sheet. Melt chocolate over hot water. Cream butter; gradually add sugar, beating until light. Add eggs separately, beating after each addition. Sift together dry ingredients. Add alternately with orange juice concentrate, beating well after each addition. Add melted chocolate chips and orange peel. Drop by teaspoonfuls about 2 inches apart onto cookie sheet. Bake until brown, about 10 minutes.

CHOCOLATE SUGAR-GLAZED COOKIES

Makes about 3 dozen

½ cup butter
½ cup shortening
1¾ cups powdered sugar, sifted
1 egg
1 teaspoon vanilla extract
¼ teaspoon almond extract
2½ cups flour, sifted

1 teaspoon baking soda
1 teaspoon cream of tartar
1 cup nuts, finely chopped
4½ ounces (¾ cup) semisweet
   chocolate chips
¼ cup light corn syrup
2 tablespoons hot water

Preheat oven to 400°. Cream butter and shortening. Gradually add powdered sugar; cream until fluffy. Add egg and vanilla and almond extracts; beat thoroughly. Sift together flour, baking soda and cream of tartar. Add to creamed mixture; beat. Stir in nuts. Drop by teaspoonfuls onto ungreased baking sheets. Bake until barely colored, 8 to 9 minutes. Cool on wire racks. Stir chocolate chips over hot water until melted. Remove from heat and stir in corn syrup and water. Spread on cooled cookies.

CHOCOLATE TEA COOKIES

Makes about 4 dozen

2½ cups flour, sifted
¾ teaspoon salt
1 cup butter, softened
1 teaspoon vanilla extract
¾ cup brown sugar, firmly packed

2 cup nuts, chopped
6 ounces (1 cup) semisweet
  chocolate chips
½ cup powdered sugar, sifted

Preheat oven to 350°. Sift together flour and salt. Beat butter with vanilla and sugar until creamy; gradually add flour mixture. Stir in nuts and chocolate chips. Form into small balls. Place on an ungreased cookie sheet. Bake about 15 minutes. While still warm, roll in powdered sugar.

CHOCOLATE-WINE COOKIES

Makes 4 dozen

1 (13½ ounces) package sugar
  cookie mix
1 egg, well beaten
¼ teaspoon nutmeg
¼ teaspoon allspice

½ teaspoon cinnamon
¼ cup sherry
4½ ounces (¾ cup) semisweet
  chocolate chips

Preheat oven to 350°. Lightly grease a cookie sheet. Mix all ingredients except chocolate chips. Melt chocolate chips over hot water; blend into batter. Drop by teaspoonfuls onto baking sheet. Bake until brown, 10 to 12 minutes.

CHUNKY CHOCOLATE CHIP DROPS

Makes about 4 dozen

3½ cups flour, sifted
1 teaspoon baking soda
½ teaspoon salt
½ teaspoon nutmeg
1 teaspoon cinnamon
⅔ cup butter
3 teaspoons vanilla extract
1 cup sugar

1 cup brown sugar, firmly packed
1 egg
½ cup sour cream
½ cup nuts, finely chopped
1½ cups raisins
9 ounces (1½ cups) semisweet
  chocolate chips

Preheat oven to 400°. Sift together first five ingredients; set aside. Beat butter and vanilla until creamy; gradually blend in sugars. Beat in egg. Stir in flour mixture, alternating with sour cream. Add nuts, raisins and chocolate chips. Drop by teaspoonfuls onto an ungreased cookie sheet. Bake until lightly browned, 15 to 18 minutes.

■

FROSTED CHOCOLATE DROPS

Makes about 5 dozen

½ teaspoon salt
1½ cups flour, sifted
1½ teaspoons baking powder
½ cup butter
1 cup sugar
2 eggs, beaten
2½ ounces (2½ squares) unsweetened chocolate, melted

½ cup milk
1 teaspoon vanilla extract
¾ cup nuts, finely chopped
¾ cup golden raisins
Frosting
Colored candy sprinkles (optional)

Preheat oven to 350°. Grease baking sheets. Mix and sift first three ingredients; set aside. Beat butter until creamy; gradually add sugar. Continue beating until light. Add eggs and melted chocolate, beating well. Stir in remaining ingredients. Add sifted dry ingredients, mixing well. Cover. Chill 1 hour. Drop by rounded teaspoonfuls onto baking sheets, about 2 to 3 inches apart. Bake until lightly browned, 10 to 13 minutes. Remove from sheets; cool on wire racks. Spread with frosting of choice. Decorate with colored candy sprinkles.

■

CHOCOLATE-RASPBERRY COOKIES

Makes about 8 dozen

2 cups flour
1 teaspoon baking powder
¼ cup cocoa
½ teaspoon baking soda
½ teaspoon salt

½ cup butter
1 cup sugar
1 egg
1 cup frozen raspberries, thawed
½ cup nuts, chopped

Preheat oven to 350°. Sift together first five ingredients. Cream butter and sugar well. Beat in egg. Add half the dry mixture to creamed mixture, stirring well. Carefully fold in raspberries. Add remaining flour and nuts. Drop by teaspoonfuls onto an ungreased baking sheet. Bake 13 to 14 minutes.

RAINBOW CHOCOLATE CHIP COOKIES

Makes about 3 dozen

1 cup plus 2 tablespoons flour,
 sifted
½ teaspoon salt
⅓ teaspoon baking soda
½ cup butter, softened
¼ cup brown sugar, firmly packed
½ cup sugar

½ teaspoon vanilla extract
¼ teaspoon water
1 egg
6 ounces (1 cup) semisweet
 chocolate chips
1 cup mixed candied fruits, finely
 chopped

Preheat oven to 375°. Grease a cookie sheet. Sift together dry ingredients. Blend butter, sugars and vanilla. Beat in egg. Add sifted dry ingredients; mix well. Stir in chocolate chips and candied fruits. Drop by teaspoonfuls onto cookie sheet. Flatten slightly with back of spoon. Bake until brown, about 10 minutes.

CHOCOLATE CHIP NUT FRIES

Tired of the basic chocolate chip cookie? Try these.
Makes 5 dozen

2 eggs
½ cup sugar
3 tablespoons butter
2½ cups flour
2½ teaspoons baking powder
¾ cup milk
1 teaspoon vanilla or almond
 extract

3 ounces (½ cup) semisweet
 chocolate chips
¼ cup nuts, finely chopped
 Oil for frying
 Powdered sugar

Beat eggs; add sugar and butter; beat until well blended. Sift dry ingredients together. Add alternately with milk to egg mixture, beating well after each addition. Stir in vanilla or almond extract, chocolate chips and nuts. Drop by rounded teaspoonfuls into a deep fryer, with cooking oil that has been heated to 365°. Fry until golden brown, about 4 minutes; drain on paper towels. When cool, roll in powdered sugar.

CHOCOLATE CHIP COOKIES

The basic, always perfect, chocolate chip cookie.
Makes 3½ dozen

½ cup butter	½ teaspoon baking soda
⅔ cup sugar	½ teaspoon salt
1 egg	2 teaspoons baking powder
1½ teaspoons vanilla extract	3 ounces (½ cup) semisweet
1½ cups flour	chocolate chips
¾ cup milk	½ cup nuts, chopped fine

Preheat oven to 375°. Combine butter, sugar, egg and vanilla in a large mixing bowl; beat until light and fluffy at highest speed of mixer. Add flour, then milk and dry ingredients, except chocolate chips and nuts. Beat about 3 minutes at low speed until well mixed (dough will be soft). Stir in chocolate chips and nuts. Drop by teaspoonfuls about 3 inches apart on ungreased baking sheet. Bake until light brown, 12 to 13 minutes.

CHOCOLATE CHIP DATE COOKIES

Dates make the difference in these.
Makes about 4 dozen

1 cup flour	1 egg, well beaten
½ teaspoon baking soda	4½ ounces (¾ cup) semisweet
½ teaspoon salt	chocolate chips
½ cup butter	1 teaspoon vanilla extract
½ cup sugar	¼ cup nuts, finely chopped
¼ cup brown sugar, firmly packed	½ cup dates, chopped

Preheat oven to 375°. Sift flour once. Measure, add soda and salt; sift again. Cream butter; gradually add sugars. Cream together until light and fluffy. Add egg and beat well again. Add flour mixture in two parts, mixing well each time. Add chocolate chips and vanilla; mix thoroughly. Add nuts and dates; blend well. Drop by teaspoonfuls about 2 inches apart onto an ungreased cookie sheet. Bake 10 to 12 minutes.

CHOCOLATE BONBONS

Makes 5½ dozen

6 ounces (1 cup) chocolate chips
½ cup butter, softened
½ cup vegetable shortening
½ teaspoon vanilla extract
1 cup sugar

1¾ cups flour, sifted
¾ teaspoon baking powder
½ cup almonds, chopped very fine
¼ cup nuts, ground

Preheat oven to 375°. Melt chocolate over hot, not boiling, water; remove and set aside. Combine butter, shortening and vanilla; beat until creamy. Gradually add sugar, beating into butter mixture. Sift together dry ingredients; blend into butter mixture. Stir in chocolate and nuts. Form into 1-inch balls; roll in ground nuts. Place on ungreased baking sheet. Bake about 10 minutes.

CHOCOLATE GRAHAM COOKIES

Makes about 2½ dozen

6 ounces (1 cup) semisweet
   chocolate chips

¼ cup sour cream
Graham crackers

Melt chocolate chips over boiling water. Add sour cream. Stir until smooth. Spread over graham crackers.

FUDGE NUT BALLS

Makes about 4 dozen

6 ounces (1 cup) semisweet
   chocolate chips
3 tablespoons light corn syrup
½ cup orange juice
1 cup nuts, finely chopped

½ cup powdered sugar, sifted
2½ cups vanilla wafers, finely
   crushed
½ cup sugar, sifted

Melt chocolate over hot, not boiling, water. Remove from heat; stir in corn syrup and orange juice. Stir in nuts, powdered sugar and crushed wafers. Let stand about ½ hour. Form into small balls, then roll in sifted sugar.

CHOCOLATE GINGERBREAD COOKIES

Makes about 4 dozen

½ cup butter
½ cup molasses
2 ounces (2 squares) unsweetened
   chocolate
2½ cups flour
1 cup sugar
1 teaspoon baking powder

½ teaspoon baking soda
1 teaspoon ginger
¼ teaspoon salt
¼ cup milk

Frosting of choice

Preheat oven to 375°. Mix butter, molasses and chocolate over hot water until blended, stirring occasionally; cool. Sift together dry ingredients; add to chocolate mixture. Add milk; mix well. Chill until firm. Roll out on lightly floured board to about ⅛-inch thickness. Cut with cookie cutter. Place on ungreased cookie sheet. Bake until crisp, about 6 minutes. Frost with frosting of choice.

Rolled and Filled Cookies

CHOCOLATE MARBLE COOKIES

Makes 3 dozen

½ cup butter
⅓ cup sugar
1 teaspoon vanilla extract

1¼ cups flour
1 ounce (1 square) unsweetened
   chocolate, melted

Preheat oven to 350°. Grease a baking sheet. Cream butter and sugar; add vanilla. Add flour and mix well. Divide dough into two parts. Melt chocolate over hot water; add this to ½ of the dough, mixing well. Roll each half into rectangular piece, about ⅛-inch thick, on a lightly floured board. Place chocolate dough on top of vanilla dough; roll up long side jelly-roll style. Fold in half and press together. Cut roll in half. Shape into two rolls 2-inches across; wrap in waxed paper. Chill a few hours. Slice into rounds ¼-inch thick. Place on baking sheet. Bake about 12 minutes.

OATMEAL CHOCOLATE STICKS

Makes about 2½ dozen

DOUGH
- 1 cup butter
- ⅔ cup brown sugar, firmly packed
- ½ cup chocolate-flavored malted milk powder
- 2¼ cups flour
- 2½ cups ground rolled oats
- 2 teaspoons baking powder
- ½ teaspoon salt
- ½ cup water

FILLING
- 2 cups dates, chopped
- 1 cup sugar
- ½ cup boiling water
- 3 tablespoons lemon juice
- 3 tablespoons orange juice

Preheat oven to 350°. Grease a baking pan. To make filling, cook dates, sugar and water to a paste. Cool. Add fruit juices; set aside. For dough, cream butter and sugar thoroughly; blend in malted milk powder. Mix and sift dry ingredients; add alternately with water to creamed mixture. Divide dough into two parts. Spread half in thin layer in bottom of baking pan. Cover with layer of filling, then spread remaining half on top. Bake until light brown, about 15 minutes. Cut into 1 × 3-inch strips.

CHOCOLATE MINT COOKIES

Makes 4 dozen

- 1½ cups flour
- ½ teaspoon baking soda
- ¼ teaspoon salt
- ½ cup butter
- ½ cup sugar
- ¼ cup brown sugar, firmly packed
- 1 egg
- 1 tablespoon water
- ½ teaspoon vanilla extract
- 48 solid chocolate mint wafers
- 24 nuts, halved

Preheat oven to 375°. Grease a cookie sheet. Mix all ingredients except mint wafers. Place in refrigerator for 2 hours. Enclose a chocolate mint wafer in each tablespoon of dough. Place 2 inches apart on cookie sheet. Top cookies with nuts. Bake until lightly browned, 10 to 12 minutes.

DELECTABLE CHOCOLATE DELIGHT COOKIES

Makes 4 dozen

1½ cups brown sugar, firmly packed
1 cup plus 2 tablespoons butter
2 tablespoons water
12 ounces (2 cups) semisweet chocolate chips
2 eggs

3 cups flour, sifted
1⅛ teaspoons salt
1¼ teaspoons baking soda
3 cups powdered sugar, sifted
¼ teaspoon peppermint extract
¼ cup whipping cream

Preheat oven to 350°. Grease a cookie sheet. Mix brown sugar and ¾ cup butter in pan. Stir over medium heat until butter is melted; stir in water. Add chocolate chips; stir until melted. Beat in eggs. Sift together dry ingredients except powdered sugar. Add to chocolate mixture, stirring after each addition. Drop by teaspoonfuls onto cookie sheet. Bake 8 to 9 minutes. Cool. To make filling, mix 2 cups powdered sugar, remaining butter, ⅛ teaspoon salt and peppermint extract; beat until light and fluffy. Blend in remaining powdered sugar, alternating with whipping cream. Place filling between two cookies to form a sandwich.

CHOCOLATE NUT-MINT SANDWICHES

Professional-looking cream-filled sandwiches and *they're terrific.*
Makes about 3 dozen

1 cup sugar
⅔ cup butter
1 egg
1 teaspoon vanilla extract
1/16 teaspoon peppermint extract
1½ cups flour, sifted
½ cup cocoa

½ teaspoon salt
½ teaspoon baking soda
1 cup nuts, finely chopped
Chocolate Mint Filling (see following recipe)

Preheat oven to 375°. Cream sugar and butter until light and fluffy. Add egg, vanilla and mint extract; mix well. Sift together dry ingredients; stir into creamed mixture. Add nuts; mix well. Chill dough about 3 hours in refrigerator. Shape into rolls about 1½ inches in diameter. Wrap in waxed paper. Chill until ready to bake. Slice very thin. Place on ungreased baking sheets. Bake about 10 minutes. Cool on wire racks. Sandwich some Chocolate Mint Filling between pairs of cookies.

CHOCOLATE MINT FILLING

Makes about 3 cups

3 ounces (½ cup) semisweet
    chocolate chips, melted
3 tablespoons butter, softened

2½ cups powdered sugar, sifted
3 tablespoons milk
⅛ teaspoon peppermint extract

Combine all ingredients; beat until smooth and creamy.

·

CHOCOLATE PEANUT BUTTER COOKIES

Makes about 8 dozen

½ cup sugar
½ cup brown sugar, firmly packed
1¼ cups flour, sifted
½ teaspoon baking soda
½ teaspoon salt

½ cup butter
½ cup peanut butter
1 egg
4½ ounces (¾ cup) semisweet
    chocolate chips, melted

Preheat oven to 375°. Mix sugars with sifted flour, soda and salt. Cream butter and peanut butter; blend in egg. Add chocolate chips. Mix both mixtures together. Roll in waxed paper until about 24 inches long. Chill about 1 hour. Cut into ¼-inch slices and place on ungreased cookie sheets. Bake 10 to 12 minutes.

·

HOLIDAY CHOCOLATE COOKIES

These make charming holiday gifts.
Makes 4 dozen

1 cup butter
1 cup sugar
1 ounce (1 square) unsweetened
    chocolate, melted
2 eggs
2 teaspoons vanilla extract
2½ cups flour
2 teaspoons cinnamon

½ teaspoon nutmeg
⅛ teaspoon allspice
½ teaspoon baking powder
½ teaspoon salt
2 egg whites
Sliced citron (garnish)
Candied cherries, chopped
    (garnish)

Preheat oven to 350°. Grease a baking sheet. Cream butter and sugar; add melted chocolate. Add eggs one at a time, beating after each addition. Add vanilla. Sift together dry ingredients; mix well into chocolate mixture. Wrap in waxed paper; chill until firm. Roll out dough on a lightly floured board to about ¼-inch thickness. Cut about 2-inch diameters with cookie cutter. Place on cookie sheet. Bake about 15 minutes. Immediately after taking from oven, brush tops with egg white. Decorate with sliced citron and bits of candied cherries. Return to oven about 5 minutes to set garnish.

GRAHAM CRACKER SANDWICHES

S'mores with peppermint.

Graham crackers　　　　　　**Marshmallow cream**
Milk chocolate bars　　　　　**Peppermint extract**

Spread graham crackers on a cookie sheet. Break chocolate bars into squares; place on graham crackers. Blend marshmallow cream with enough peppermint extract to flavor lightly. Using a teaspoon, drop some flavored marshmallow cream on top of each chocolate-covered graham cracker. Broil a moment or two until marshmallow is slightly toasted and chocolate softened. Place another cracker on top of each to make a sandwich. Serve two or three per person.

CHOCOLATE SOUR CREAM REFRIGERATOR COOKIES

Makes about 12 dozen

1 cup butter　　　　　　　　　　　　**3 cups flour**
½ cup brown sugar, firmly packed　　**¼ teaspoon baking soda**
1 cup sugar　　　　　　　　　　　　**1 teaspoon salt**
½ cup sour cream　　　　　　　　　　**1 teaspoon baking powder**
2½ ounces (2½ squares) semisweet　　**1 teaspoon vanilla extract**
**　chocolate, melted**

Preheat oven to 400°. Cream butter and sugars thoroughly; stir in sour cream and melted chocolate. Mix and sift dry ingredients; add to chocolate mixture. Stir in vanilla. Chill. Shape into roll; wrap in waxed paper. Refrigerate overnight. Slice very thin. Place on ungreased cookie sheet. Bake 8 minutes.

CHOCOLATE PRETZEL COOKIES

Wonderful looking and fun to make.
Makes 2 to 4 dozen, depending on size

1 cup butter
⅔ cup sugar
1 egg, well beaten
2 ounces (2 squares) unsweetened
   chocolate, melted

1½ cups flour, sifted
½ teaspoon cinnamon
¼ teaspoon allspice
1 cup nuts, finely chopped

Preheat oven to 350°. Cream butter until soft; gradually beat in sugar until mixture is not grainy. Beat in egg. Sift dry ingredients together; add to mixture. Refrigerate overnight. When ready to bake, take out a small amount of dough, leaving remainder in refrigerator to use when needed.* With hands, roll dough to about ½-inch thickness. Shape into pretzels. Place on an ungreased cookie sheet. Bake about 10 minutes. Cool a little, then roll in nuts.

*If dough is wrapped well in waxed paper, it will keep in refrigerator 6 or 7 days.

CHAPTER THREE

CAKES AND TORTES

Cakes

DARK & MOIST CHOCOLATE CAKE

A basic, two-layer chocolate cake.
Makes one 2-layer, 8-inch cake

3 ounces (3 squares) unsweetened
  chocolate
1¼ cups sugar
1¼ cups milk
1 egg yolk, beaten slightly
1¾ cups flour, sifted
2 teaspoons baking powder

¼ teaspoon salt
½ teaspoon baking soda
⅓ cup butter
1 egg, beaten slightly
1 teaspoon vanilla extract
Frosting of choice

Preheat oven to 350°. Grease well two 8-inch cake pans. Blend chocolate, ¼ cup sugar and ½ cup milk over hot water; cook slowly, stirring occasionally. Stir slowly into egg yolk; mix well. Cool. Mix flour, baking powder, salt and soda together and sift three times. Cream butter until soft. Gradually add remaining sugar, creaming after each addition until light and fluffy. Add egg; beat well. Add chocolate mixture which has been cooled. Add flour alternately with remaining milk, a little at a time; beat after each addition until smooth. Add vanilla. Pour into pans; bake until tester inserted in center of cake comes out clean, about 30 minutes. Cool. Frost with frosting of choice.

ALBUQUERQUE
CHOCOLATE CAKE

Extra rich. A little whipped cream is the perfect accompaniment.
Makes one single-layer, 8-inch square cake

6 eggs, separated
4 tablespoons sugar
6 ounces sweet cooking chocolate
1 tablespoon water

1 teaspoon vanilla extract
⅔ cup flour, sifted
1 tablespoon arrowroot
1 cup whipping cream, whipped

Preheat oven to 375°. Grease an 8-inch square pan, which is at least 4 inches high. Beat egg yolks until thick and lemon colored. Add sugar a tablespoon at a time, beating well after each addition. Melt chocolate and water together over hot water, in the top of a double boiler. Remove from heat; cool. Beat chocolate into egg mixture; blend well. Beat in vanilla. Sift flour and arrowroot powder together; add to batter. Mix well. Beat egg whites until very stiff; fold into batter. Pour sugar over bottom of pan, being sure to coat evenly; pour in batter over sugar. Bake until cake tester inserted in center of cake comes out clean, about 30 minutes. Cool in pan 30 minutes; remove. Serve with whipped cream.

SUE'S CHOCOLATE CAKE

Makes one 2-layer, 8-inch cake

2 *cups brown sugar, firmly packed*	3 *eggs, well beaten*
½ *cup milk*	2 *cups flour*
3 *ounces (3 squares) unsweetened* *chocolate*	¼ *teaspoon salt*
	1 *teaspoon baking soda*
½ *cup butter*	½ *cup milk*
1 *teaspoon vanilla extract*	*Frosting of choice*

Preheat oven to 350°. Grease two 8-inch cake pans. Heat 1 cup brown sugar, ½ cup milk and chocolate in top of double boiler until chocolate is melted; cool. Cream butter, vanilla and remaining sugar. Sift together dry ingredients; add to eggs. Add alternately with milk to creamed mixture. Add chocolate mixture. Pour into pans. Bake until tester inserted in center comes out clean, about 30 minutes. Frost and fill with frosting of choice.

CHOCOLATE SOUR CREAM CAKE

Great served warm or cold.
Makes one single-layer, 9 × 13-inch cake

6 *tablespoons butter, softened*	1½ *teaspoons baking powder*
1 *cup plus 1 tablespoon sugar*	1⅓ *cups flour*
2 *eggs*	1 *cup sour cream*
1 *teaspoon cinnamon*	4½ *ounces (¾ cup) semisweet*
1 *teaspoon baking soda*	*chocolate chips*

Preheat oven to 350°. Grease and flour a 9 × 13-inch baking pan. Mix butter and sugar until well blended. Beat in eggs, one at a time. Stir in dry ingredients, blending well with butter mixture. Add sour cream. Pour batter into pan. Scatter chocolate chips evenly over batter, then sprinkle with remaining sugar. Bake until cake begins to shrink from sides of pan, 45 to 50 minutes. Serve warm or cool, but do not place in refrigerator.

NEW JERSEY
CHOCOLATE BIRTHDAY CAKE

Mayonnaise lends a light touch to this cake.
Makes one single-layer, 8 × 10-inch cake

2 cups flour, sifted
½ teaspoon salt
1 cup sugar
⅓ cup cocoa
1 teaspoon baking soda

1 cup water
2 teaspoons vanilla extract
1 teaspoon almond extract
⅔ cup mayonnaise
Chocolate frosting of choice

Preheat oven to 350°. Grease an 8 × 10 × 2-inch pan; line with waxed paper. Sift together dry ingredients into a bowl. Add remaining ingredients. Stir until well blended. Pour into pan. Bake until tester inserted in center comes out clean, about 45 minutes. Cool 5 minutes in pan; complete cooling on a wire rack. Frost with chocolate frosting of choice.

HARRY'S FAVORITE
CHOCOLATE CAKE

Makes one single-layer, 9 × 9-inch cake

½ cup butter
1½ cups sugar
2 eggs, beaten
1 teaspoon vanilla extract
1 teaspoon baking powder
1 teaspoon salt

1¾ cups flour, sifted
½ cup sour milk*
½ cup cocoa
1 teaspoon baking soda
½ cup boiling water
Frosting of choice

Preheat oven to 350°. Line a 9-inch square pan with waxed paper; grease both pan and paper. Cream butter, adding sugar gradually. Beat until light. Add beaten eggs and vanilla to creamed mixture and beat until fluffy. Sift together baking powder, salt and flour; add about half of this mixture and ¼ cup sour milk to creamed mixture. Beat until smooth. Add remaining flour and sour milk; beat until smooth. Mix cocoa and baking soda; stir in boiling water until smooth. Add to batter, mixing well. Pour into pan. Bake until tester inserted in center comes out clean, about 45 minutes. Cool in pan 20 minutes; remove. Cool completely and frost with frosting of choice.

*See Bett's Chocolate Cake, page 64.

GERMAN CHOCOLATE CAKE

An Old World favorite.
Makes one 3-layer, 8- or 9-inch cake

8 ounces sweet chocolate	¹⁄₁₆ teaspoon salt
½ cup boiling water	1 teaspoon baking soda
1 cup butter	2½ cups flour, sifted
2 cups sugar	1 cup buttermilk
4 eggs, separated	Chocolate Coconut Pecan
1 teaspoon vanilla extract	Frosting (see following recipe)
½ teaspoon black walnut flavoring	

Preheat oven to 350°. Grease and line bottoms of three 8- or 9-inch cake pans with waxed paper. Melt chocolate in boiling water; cool. Cream butter and sugar together until light and fluffy; add egg yolks, beating well after each addition. Add black walnut flavoring to chocolate mixture; add chocolate mixture to batter. Sift together dry ingredients; add alternately with buttermilk to chocolate batter. Beat until smooth; fold in egg whites, which have been beaten until stiff. Pour batter into pans. Bake until tester inserted in center of cake comes out clean, 30 to 40 minutes. Cool 20 minutes in pans; complete cooling on wire racks. Frost with Chocolate Coconut Pecan Frosting.

CHOCOLATE COCONUT PECAN FROSTING

Makes about 5 cups

1 cup evaporated milk	1 teaspoon vanilla extract
1 cup sugar	1⅓ cups coconut, shredded
3 egg yolks	1 to 2 teaspoons cocoa
½ cup butter	1 cup nuts, chopped

Combine milk, sugar, egg yolks, butter and vanilla in saucepan. Cook, stirring constantly, over medium heat until thick, 10 to 12 minutes. Add coconut and nuts. Beat until frosting is cool and thick enough to spread on cake.

DARK RUSSIAN CHOCOLATE CAKE

Makes one 10-inch Bundt cake

2½ cups flour, sifted
1 teaspoon baking soda
¼ teaspoon salt
1 cup butter
2 cups sugar
4 eggs

1 cup buttermilk
¾ cup cocoa
⅔ cup boiling water
2 teaspoons almond or vanilla
   extract
Frosting of choice

Preheat oven to 375°. Grease and flour well one 10-inch Bundt pan. Sift together first three ingredients. Cream butter and sugar at medium speed of electric mixer until fluffy. Add eggs, one at a time; beat well after each addition. Beat in buttermilk and flour mixture alternately. Stir cocoa into ⅔ cup boiling water until dissolved. Beat cocoa mixture and vanilla or almond extract into batter at low speed of mixer; pour batter into pan. Bake until cake tester inserted in center comes out clean, about 60 minutes. Cool cake 5 to 10 minutes; invert onto wire rack. Frost with frosting of choice.

BETT'S CHOCOLATE CAKE

Makes one 2-layer, 9-inch cake

2 cups flour, sifted
1 teaspoon baking soda
½ teaspoon salt
½ cup butter
1 cup sugar
1 egg, well beaten

⅓ cup water
½ cup cocoa
1 cup sour milk*
1 teaspoon vanilla extract
Bett's Chocolate Icing (see
   following recipe)

Preheat oven to 325°. Grease two 9-inch cake pans. Sift flour once. Add baking soda and salt; sift three times. Cream butter; add sugar gradually. Beat until fluffy; add egg. Add water to cocoa slowly, making a smooth paste. Add to creamed mixture, blending well. Add flour in small amounts, alternating with milk. Beat until smooth; add vanilla. Bake until tester inserted in center comes out clean, about 50 minutes. Cool in pans 20 minutes; remove. Ice with Bett's Chocolate Icing.

*To sour milk add 1 tablespoon white vinegar or lemon juice to 1 cup of milk. Let stand at room temperature 10 to 15 minutes.

BETT'S CHOCOLATE ICING

Makes about 1¼ cups

1 cup powdered sugar
2 tablespoons cocoa
1 teaspoon vanilla extract

⅛ cup milk
2 tablespoons butter

Mix together all ingredients. Beat until mixture reaches spreading consistency.

•

ST. PADDY'S CHOCOLATE CAKE

A spicy, Irish version of the chocolate sour cream cake.
Makes one 2-layer, 8-inch cake

1½ cups flour, sifted
½ teaspoon salt
¾ teaspoon cinnamon
½ teaspoon allspice
¼ teaspoon ground cloves
1 teaspoon baking powder
⅓ cup butter
¾ cup sugar
3 eggs, separated

⅓ cup sour cream
¼ cup hot water
1 teaspoon baking soda
4 ounces (4 squares) semisweet
   chocolate, melted
1½ teaspoons vanilla extract
   Boiled icing, tinted green or
   frosting of choice

Preheat oven to 350°. Grease two 8-inch cake pans. Mix and sift together first six ingredients three times. Cream butter until soft; gradually add sugar, beating after each addition until light and fluffy. Add egg yolks, which have been beaten until thick. Add sour cream; blend well. Add hot water mixed with baking soda, then chocolate, beating until well blended. Add flour mixture; beat until smooth. Fold in unbeaten whites; add vanilla. Pour into pans. Bake until tester inserted in center comes out clean, about 30 minutes. Cool in pans 5 minutes; then cool on wire racks. Frost with boiled icing or frosting of choice.

•

DES MOINES
CHOCOLATE SOUR CREAM CAKE

The sour cream flavor is enhanced with coffee.
Makes one 2-layer, 8-inch cake

1 cup sugar
1 teaspoon salt
2 eggs, well beaten
1½ cups flour, sifted
1 teaspoon baking soda

1 cup sour cream
2 ounces (2 squares) unsweetened chocolate
2 cups hot coffee, double strength
Frosting of choice

Preheat oven to 350°. Grease well two 8-inch cake pans. Combine sugar, salt and eggs; beat well. Sift together flour and soda; add to egg mixture alternately with sour cream. Melt chocolate in hot coffee; add to batter. Pour into pans. Bake until tester inserted in center comes out clean, approximately 30 minutes. Cool in pans 5 minutes; cool completely on wire racks. Frost.

"IKE" EISENHOWER'S
BIRTHDAY CAKE

This recipe came from Ike's niece.
Makes one 2-layer, 9-inch cake

2½ cups flour, sifted
¼ teaspoon salt
1 teaspoon baking powder (rounded)
½ cup butter
2 cups sugar

3 eggs, separated
1 teaspoon vanilla extract
⅔ cup cocoa
½ cup boiling water
1 cup sour milk
Frosting of choice

Preheat oven to 375°. Grease two 9-inch cake pans. Sift together flour and baking powder. Cream butter and slowly beat in sugar. Add egg yolks and vanilla, then cocoa, which has been dissolved in boiling water. Add flour mixture alternately with sour milk. Carefully fold in egg whites, which have been beaten until stiff. Pour into pans. Bake until tester inserted in center of cake comes out clean, about 25 minutes. Cool in pans 20 minutes; complete cooling on wire racks. Frost with frosting of choice.

VELVETY CHOCOLATE CAKE

Subtly flavored with coffee and buttermilk.
Makes one 2-layer, 8- or 9-inch cake

6 ounces (1 cup) semisweet
  chocolate chips
1¾ cups flour, sifted
1 teaspoon instant coffee
2½ teaspoons baking powder
1 teaspoon salt

1¼ cups brown sugar, firmly packed
1⅓ cups buttermilk
½ cup butter, softened
1½ teaspoons vanilla extract
1 egg
Frosting of choice

Preheat oven to 375°. Grease sides of two 8- or 9-inch cake pans and line bottoms with waxed paper. Melt chocolate over hot, not boiling, water; remove from heat. Sift together flour, coffee, baking powder, soda and salt. Add brown sugar, 1 cup buttermilk, butter and vanilla; beat 3 minutes at medium speed of mixer. Scrape bowl and beaters as needed. Add melted chocolate, remaining buttermilk and egg. Pour into pans. Bake until tester inserted in center comes out clean, about 30 minutes. Cool 10 minutes. Remove from pans; continue cooling on wire racks. Fill and frost with frosting of choice.

GEORGIA CHOCOLATE CAKE

An American classic with the delicate flavor of buttermilk.
Makes one 2-layer, 9-inch cake

4 ounces sweet chocolate
½ cup boiling water
1 cup butter
2 cups sugar
4 eggs, separated
1 teaspoon vanilla extract

2½ cups flour
½ teaspoon salt
1 teaspoon baking soda
1 cup buttermilk
Frosting of choice

Preheat oven to 350°. Line bottoms of two 9-inch cake pans with waxed paper. Melt chocolate in boiling water; cool. Cream butter and sugar until fluffy; add egg yolks one at a time, beating well after each addition. Add melted chocolate and vanilla; mix well. Sift together dry ingredients. Add alternately with buttermilk to chocolate mixture, beating well after each addition until smooth. Fold in egg whites, which have been beaten until stiff. Pour batter into pans. Bake until tester inserted in center comes out clean, 35 to 40 minutes. Cool in pans 20 minutes; complete cooling on wire racks. Frost tops with frosting of choice.

PHILADELPHIA CHOCOLATE SPICE CAKE

Makes one 2-layer, 9-inch cake

¾ cup butter
1½ cups sugar
3 eggs, well beaten
1¾ cups flour
½ teaspoon baking powder
½ teaspoon baking soda
½ teaspoon salt
¾ teaspoon nutmeg

½ teaspoon cinnamon
¼ teaspoon allspice
2 tablespoons cocoa
¾ cup buttermilk
1 teaspoon vanilla extract
1 teaspoon lemon extract
½ cup nuts, coarsely chopped
Frosting of choice

Preheat oven to 350°. Grease well and flour two 9-inch cake pans. Cream butter; add sugar gradually. Blend in eggs. Sift together dry ingredients; add alternately with buttermilk to creamed mixture. Blend in vanilla, lemon extract and nuts. Pour into pans. Bake until tester inserted in center comes out clean, about 30 minutes. Cool in pans 5 minutes; cool completely on wire racks. Frost with frosting of choice.

FRENCH CHOCOLATE CAKE

This recipe is from my grandmother, a native of Alsace-Lorraine.
Makes one 2-layer, 8-inch cake

4 ounces (4 squares) unsweetened
  chocolate
¼ cup plus 1 tablespoon water
½ cup margarine
½ cup sugar
3 eggs, separated

¼ cup nuts, finely chopped
1 tablespoon rum
⅓ cup flour, unsifted
½ teaspoon grated orange peel
½ teaspoon allspice
½ cup raspberry jam

Preheat oven to 325°. Grease and flour two 8-inch cake pans. Melt chocolate and water over low heat, stirring constantly. Add margarine and stir. When completely melted, remove from heat and blend in sugar. Cool. Add egg yolks, beating well after each addition. Fold in nuts and rum. Mix flour and remaining ingredients except egg whites and jam. Beat egg whites until stiff but not dry; fold into mixture. Pour into pans. Bake until cake tester inserted in center of cake comes out clean, 25 to 30 minutes. Invert pans on wire racks. Cool. Melt jam with remaining tablespoon of water; spread half over one cake layer. Cover this with second layer and spread remaining jam on top.

CHOCOLATE APRICOT
UPSIDE DOWN CAKE

Makes one single-layer, 9 × 9-inch cake

½ cup brown sugar, firmly packed
⅔ cup butter
2½ cups apricot halves, drained
   (reserve syrup)
⅔ cup coconut, flaked
  4 ounces sweet cooking chocolate
1½ cups cake flour, sifted
  1 cup sugar
½ teaspoon baking powder

½ teaspoon baking soda
½ teaspoon salt
¾ cup buttermilk
  1 teaspoon vanilla extract
  2 eggs
   Whipping cream, whipped
   (optional)

Preheat oven to 350°. Combine brown sugar and ⅓ cup butter. Melt over low heat, then spread evenly in a 9-inch square pan. Arrange apricot halves over brown sugar mixture, rounded sides up. Mix coconut with 2 tablespoons of reserved apricot syrup; sprinkle over apricot halves. Melt chocolate over low heat; cool. Sift together dry ingredients. Stir remaining butter to soften; add dry ingredients, ¼ cup plus 2 tablespoons buttermilk and vanilla. Mix until all flour is well moistened; beat 2 minutes at medium speed of mixer, scraping bowl occasionally. Add melted chocolate, eggs and remaining buttermilk. Beat another minute with mixer. Pour batter into pan over apricots. Bake until cake springs back when pressed lightly with finger, about 45 minutes. Let cake cool in pan about 5 minutes; invert onto serving plate. Serve warm. Top with whipped cream, if desired.

BURNT SUGAR CHOCOLATE CAKE

This has a wonderful caramel flavor.
Makes one 3-layer, 8-inch, or 2-layer, 9-inch cake

⅞ cup flour
  2 teaspoons baking powder
1½ cups sugar
½ cup butter
  2 egg yolks
  3 teaspoons caramel (see following
   recipe)

  2 tablespoons cocoa
1½ teaspoons vanilla extract
  1 cup water
  2 egg whites
   Frosting of choice

Preheat oven to 350°. Grease well two or three 8- or 9-inch cake pans. Sift together flour and baking powder; set aside ½ cup. Mix balance of flour mixture with rest of ingredients, stirring well. Add ½ cup flour mixture. Beat egg whites until stiff peaks form; fold into batter. Turn into cake pans. Bake until tester inserted in center of cake comes out clean, 25 to 30 minutes. Cool in pans 20 minutes; complete cooling on wire racks. Frost and fill with frosting of choice.

CARAMEL

1 cup sugar   ½ cup boiling water

Put sugar in a small saucepan over low heat, stirring constantly while it melts, browns and turns black. Remove from heat; add ½ cup boiling water. Return to heat; boil until it is like thin molasses. (This makes enough caramel for 3 cakes.)

CHOCOLATE CARNIVAL CAKE

Filled with a rich, nutty filling.
Makes one 2-layer, 8-inch cake

2 cups flour
1 cup brown sugar, firmly packed
3 teaspoons baking powder
1 teaspoon salt
½ teaspoon baking soda
½ cup butter
1¼ cups milk
3 eggs

1 teaspoon vanilla extract
1 teaspoon black walnut flavoring
6 ounces (½ cup) semisweet
    chocolate chips
Chocolate Nut Filling (see
    following recipe)
Chocolate frosting of choice

Preheat oven to 350°. Grease and flour two 8-inch cake pans. Measure all ingredients into a bowl. Blend on low speed of mixer about 1 minute, scraping sides of bowl constantly. Beat 3 to 4 minutes at medium speed, continuing to scrape bowl. Pour into pans. Bake until tester inserted in center of cake comes out clean, about 45 minutes. Cool. Fill layers with Chocolate Nut Filling; frost sides and top with chocolate frosting of choice.

CHOCOLATE NUT FILLING

Makes 1½ cups

¼ cup brown sugar, firmly packed
2 tablespoons flour
1 tablespoon cocoa
½ cup milk

2 tablespoons butter
½ cup nuts, chopped
1 teaspoon vanilla extract
1 teaspoon black walnut flavoring

Mix sugar, cocoa and flour in pan; stir in milk. Bring to boil, stirring constantly. Boil and stir 3 minutes. Remove from heat. Stir in butter, nuts, black walnut flavoring and vanilla, and cool.

CHOCOLATE LOAF

Orange complements chocolate perfectly in this recipe.
Makes one 5 × 9-inch loaf cake

6 ounces (1 cup) semisweet
  chocolate chips
2 cups flour, sifted
1 teaspoon baking powder
½ teaspoon salt
1 cup butter
1 teaspoon vanilla extract

¼ teaspoon nutmeg
1 cup sugar
5 eggs
¼ cup orange juice
½ cup nuts, finely chopped
1 tablespoon orange peel, grated

Preheat oven to 300°. Line a 5 × 9 × 3-inch loaf pan with waxed paper. Melt chocolate over hot, not boiling, water; remove from heat. Sift together flour, baking powder and salt. Beat butter, vanilla and nutmeg until creamy; gradually beat in sugar. Add eggs one at a time, beating after each addition. Stir in melted chocolate. Add flour mixture alternately with orange juice. Fold in nuts and grated peel. Pour into pans. Bake until top splits a little, about 1 hour and 45 minutes.

CHOCOLATE MOCHA LOAF CAKE

Makes one 5 × 9-inch loaf cake

1½ cups flour, sifted
1¼ cups sugar
1 tablespoon instant coffee
1 teaspoon salt
¼ teaspoon baking soda
½ teaspoon cream of tartar
¼ cup instant dry milk
⅔ cup butter, softened

⅔ cup water
1 teaspoon vanilla extract
½ teaspoon almond extract
3 eggs
2 ounces (2 squares) unsweetened
  chocolate
Powdered sugar (garnish)

Preheat oven to 325°. Grease and lightly flour a 5 × 9 × 3-inch loaf pan. Sift together first seven ingredients into large bowl. Add butter and beat at medium speed, until very well mixed. Stir in water and vanilla and almond extracts; beat well 3 to 4 minutes. Add eggs and chocolate, which has been melted over hot water. Beat another 2 to 3 minutes at medium speed. Pour into loaf pan; gently cut through batter with a knife to remove any air bubbles. Bake until tester inserted in center of cake comes out clean, about 75 minutes. Cool 10 minutes; remove from pan. Cool completely; sift powdered sugar over top.

YEAST CHOCOLATE CAKE

Makes one 2-layer, 8-inch cake

1 cup butter
2 cups sugar
3 eggs
1 envelope dry active yeast
¼ cup lukewarm water
1 cup milk
2 ounces (2 squares) unsweetened
 chocolate, melted

3 cups flour, sifted
½ teaspoon salt
1 teaspoon baking soda
½ cup nuts, chopped
Frosting of choice

Grease two 8-inch cake pans or one 9-inch tube pan. Cream butter and sugar until fluffy. Add eggs, one at a time, beating well after each addition. Soften yeast in water; beat into creamed mixture. Add milk, melted chocolate, dry ingredients, which have been sifted together, and nuts. Beat 5 to 6 minutes. Pour into pans. Cover with waxed paper; chill overnight in refrigerator. Remove from refrigerator. Preheat oven to 350°. Bake until tester inserted in center of cake comes out clean, about 45 minutes. Cool in pans for 45 minutes. Frost with frosting of choice.

■

CHOCOLATE CHIFFON
RUM OR BRANDY CAKE

Airy and light with a hint of liquor flavoring.
Makes one 10-inch tube cake

2 cups eggs, separated (about 6
 to 8)
½ cup cocoa, sifted
¾ cup boiling water
1¾ cups sugar
1½ teaspoons baking soda
1¾ cups flour, sifted

1 teaspoon salt
½ cup cooking oil
2 teaspoons rum or brandy
 flavoring
½ teaspoon cream of tartar
Frosting of choice or whipped
 cream

Preheat oven to 325°. Have ready an ungreased 10-inch tube pan and a wine bottle. Separate eggs; allow egg whites to reach room temperature. Combine cocoa and boiling water in a small bowl; stir until smooth; cool. Sift together dry ingredients in a large bowl; make a well in the center. Add egg yolks, oil, rum or brandy flavoring and cooled cocoa mixture; beat until smooth. Sprinkle cream of tartar into egg whites; beat until very stiff peaks form. Pour batter over whites; stir and fold gently with a rubber spatula until just blended. Pour into pan. Bake until tester comes out clean, about 60 minutes. Balance tube pan on top of wine bottle until completely cool. Carefully remove pan. Frost with frosting of choice or serve with whipped cream.

CHOCOLATE SURPRISE CAKE

A memorable cake traditionally tinted with red food coloring.
Makes one 9-inch tube cake

2 eggs	½ teaspoon salt
⅓ cup butter	1 teaspoon baking soda
1¼ cups sugar	1¼ cups milk
2 cups flour	1 teaspoon vanilla extract
½ cup cocoa	1 teaspoon red food coloring
1 package dry active yeast	(optional)
1 tablespoon baking powder	Frosting of choice (optional)

Preheat oven to 375°. Grease a 9-inch tube pan. Combine eggs, butter and sugar; beat well about 2 minutes at high speed of mixer, scraping sides of bowl often. Add flour and remaining ingredients (yeast does not need to be softened). Blend well at low speed; beat 5 minutes at medium speed. Scrape sides of bowl frequently. Spread batter in pan. Cover with a towel and place in a warm spot for 30 minutes. Cover with foil. Bake about 15 minutes; remove foil and bake another 15 to 20 minutes or until cake tester inserted in center of cake comes out clean. Invert at once onto wire rack. Cool. Frost if desired with frosting of choice.

CHOCOLATE CHEESE CAKE

A dense, marbleized cheesecake in a graham cracker crust.
Makes one single-layer, 9-inch cake

3 cups cream cheese, softened
1 cup sugar, scant
1½ tablespoons arrowroot
½ teaspoon black walnut flavoring
½ teaspoon vanilla extract

3 eggs
1 ounce (1 square) unsweetened
  chocolate, melted
1 cup graham cracker crumbs
3 tablespoons butter

Preheat oven to 350°. Lightly grease a 9-inch springform pan. Combine cheese, all but ¼ cup sugar, arrowroot powder, vanilla extract and black walnut flavoring. When well blended add eggs, one at a time, beating well after each addition. Add melted chocolate to 1 cup of the batter, mixing well. Combine crumbs, melted butter and remaining sugar. Press into bottom and sides of pan to form a crust. Bake for 10 to 12 minutes. Spoon chocolate and plain batter alternately into crust; cut through batter with knife to marbleize. Increase oven temperature to 450°; bake for 10 to 12 minutes. Reduce heat to 250° for 30 minutes. Cool. Run knife around rim and cool for at least 1 hour before removing rim. (Bottom of springform pan may be left under cake and set on serving plate; this will prevent cake from breaking when transferring to plate.)

FESTIVE CHOCOLATE FRUIT CAKE

Makes one 10-inch tube cake or about 8 miniature cakes

½ cup flour, sifted
½ teaspoon salt
½ teaspoon baking soda
6 ounces (1 cup) semisweet
  chocolate chips
⅓ cup butter
1 teaspoon lemon or orange extract

¼ cup brown sugar, firmly packed
3 eggs
¼ cup water
1¾ to 2 cups mixed candied fruit,
  finely chopped
1 cup nuts, finely chopped

Preheat oven to 350°. Grease and flour a 1½ quart ring mold or 8 miniature loaf pans. Sift together dry ingredients; set aside. Melt chocolate chips over hot, not boiling, water; remove from heat. Thoroughly cream butter, lemon or orange extract and brown sugar; beat in eggs one at a time. Stir in melted chocolate. Add flour mixture alternately with water. Fold in fruit and nuts. Pour into mold or loaf pans. Bake until tester inserted in center comes out clean, about 35 minutes. Cool 5 minutes in mold or loaf pans; turn out onto wire racks.

CHOCOLATE TEA RING

Makes the most informal get-together a special occasion.
Makes one 10-inch tea ring

2 cups flour
3 teaspoons baking powder
½ teaspoon salt
¼ cup plus 3 tablespoons butter
1 cup milk
3 ounces (½ cup) semisweet
   chocolate chips

1⅓ cups coconut, shredded
2 tablespoons sugar
¼ teaspoon cinnamon
⅛ teaspoon allspice
   Glaze of choice

Preheat oven to 375°. Grease well a baking sheet. Sift together flour, baking powder and salt. Cut in ¼ cup butter until consistency of small peas. Add sufficient milk to make a soft dough. Roll out to a 10 × 6½ × ¼-inch rectangle. Sprinkle chocolate chips, coconut, sugar, cinnamon and allspice over dough. Roll up long side jelly-roll style; moisten and seal edges. Form into a ring on baking sheet. Cut gashes in top of ring about 1-inch apart. Bake about 45 minutes. Spoon glaze of choice over ring. Serve hot.

CHOCOLATE PEAR CAKE

Makes one single-layer, 9 × 9-inch cake

2 cups flour, sifted
½ cup sugar
¼ cup cocoa
2 teaspoons baking powder
¼ teaspoon baking soda
1 teaspoon allspice

1 teaspoon salt
2 pears
1 egg
¾ cup milk
¼ cup butter, melted

Preheat oven to 350°. Grease and flour a 9-inch square cake pan. Sift together dry ingredients. Dice enough pear to make 1 cup. Stir pear into flour mixture. Blend egg, milk and butter; add all at once to flour mixture. Stir until smooth. Pour into pan. Bake until tester inserted in center of cake comes out clean, 45 to 50 minutes.

CHOCOLATE ORANGE CAKE

Makes one 3-layer, 9-inch cake

1 teaspoon baking powder	2 teaspoons orange extract
1 teaspoon salt	1/2 cup orange chocolate liqueur
1 teaspoon baking soda	3/4 cup evaporated milk
2 1/4 cups flour, sifted	1/2 cup water
2/3 cup butter	1/4 cup cooking oil
1 1/2 cups sugar	Chocolate Orange Frosting (see
3 eggs	following recipe)
3 ounces (3 squares) unsweetened	Nut halves (optional)
chocolate, melted	

Preheat oven to 350°. Grease and lightly flour three 9-inch cake pans. Sift together dry ingredients; set aside. Cream butter and sugar until light and fluffy. Add eggs one at a time; beat well after each addition. Add melted chocolate, which has been slightly cooled, orange extract and orange chocolate liqueur; blend well. Mix together milk and water. Add dry ingredients to chocolate mixture alternately with milk mixture. Mix until smooth. Stir in cooking oil. Pour into pans. Bake until tops spring back when lightly touched with finger, about 30 minutes. Cool layers in pans about 5 minutes; turn out onto wire racks. Cool completely. Fill and frost with Chocolate Orange Frosting and garnish with nuts.

CHOCOLATE ORANGE FROSTING

Makes about 2 1/2 cups

1/2 cup cream cheese, whipped	1/4 teaspoon orange extract
2 tablespoons orange chocolate	2 cups powdered sugar
liqueur	Grated peels from 2 oranges

Beat cream cheese until fluffy; beat in orange chocolate liqueur and orange extract until well blended. Gradually beat in sugar; add grated orange peel.

NOUGAT-FILLED CHOCOLATE CAKE

A creamy nougat filling makes this very special.
Makes one 2-layer, 8-inch cake

2 cups flour, sifted
½ teaspoon baking powder
⅛ teaspoon salt
1 teaspoon baking soda
½ cup butter
1 cup sugar
1 egg
2 egg yolks

3 ounces (3 squares) unsweetened
   chocolate, melted and cooled
1 cup buttermilk
1 teaspoon vanilla extract
   Chocolate Nougat Filling (see
      following recipe)

Preheat oven to 325°. Grease well two 8-inch cake pans. Mix and sift first four ingredients together three times. Cream butter; gradually add sugar. Beat until light and fluffy. Add egg and egg yolks, beating until blended. Add chocolate, mixing well. Add flour alternately with buttermilk, a small amount at a time. Beat after each addition until smooth. Add vanilla. Pour into pans. Bake until tester inserted in center comes out clean, about 30 minutes. Cool in pans 5 minutes; complete cooling on wire racks.

CHOCOLATE NOUGAT FILLING

Makes about 3 cups

¾ cup sugar
¼ cup flour
⅛ teaspoon salt
1 egg
1 cup water

2 ounces (2 squares) unsweetened
   chocolate, melted
½ teaspoon vanilla extract
¼ teaspoon almond extract
1 cup nuts, finely chopped
   (optional)

Mix sugar, flour and salt. Beat egg slightly; add water. Add to flour mixture, beating well. Add to melted chocolate. Cook over hot water until thickened. Add vanilla and almond extracts. If desired, add ½ cup finely chopped nuts. Cool.

KANSAS CITY
CHOCOLATE APPLESAUCE CAKE

Makes one 5 × 9-inch loaf cake

2 cups flour, sifted
1 teaspoon salt
1 teaspoon baking soda
¾ cup sugar
½ cup butter
1 teaspoon cinnamon
1 teaspoon ground cloves

½ teaspoon allspice
2 eggs
1 cup applesauce, canned
6 ounces (1 cup) semisweet
   chocolate chips
½ cup golden raisins
½ cup nuts, chopped

Preheat oven to 350°. Line a 5 × 9 × 3-inch loaf pan with waxed paper. Sift together dry ingredients; set aside. Beat sugar, butter and spices until creamy. Add eggs one at a time, beating well after each addition. Add flour mixture alternately with applesauce. Stir in chocolate chips, raisins and nuts. Spread in pan. Bake until tester inserted in center comes out clean, about 70 minutes. Cool in pan 10 to 12 minutes; remove from pan and cool on wire rack.

LOUISIANA HOEDOWN CAKE

Layered with coconut and flavored with coffee and sour cream.
Makes one 10-inch tube cake

4 eggs, separated
6 ounces (1 cup) semisweet
   chocolate chips
½ cup plus 1 tablespoon water
2 teaspoons vanilla extract
1 teaspoon instant coffee
1½ cups plus 6 tablespoons sugar
2 cups coconut, shredded

2 cups plus 1 tablespoon flour
¾ teaspoon salt
1 teaspoon baking soda
½ cup butter
½ cup sour cream
   Frosting of choice

Preheat oven to 350°. Grease the bottom only of a 10-inch tube pan. Combine 1 egg white, 1 tablespoon water and 1 teaspoon vanilla; beat until foamy. Beat in ½ cup sugar; continue to beat until stiff glossy peaks form. Fold in coconut, 1 tablespoon flour and ¼ teaspoon salt. Set aside. Combine chocolate chips, ½ cup water and instant coffee; melt chocolate chips. Remove from heat. Sift together 2 cups flour and baking soda and set aside. Beat 3 egg whites until foamy. Gradually add 6 tablespoons sugar, beating until stiff, glossy peaks form. Combine 1 cup sugar, ½ cup butter, 3 egg yolks, 1 teaspoon vanilla, and ½ teaspoon salt; beat until creamy. Add flour mixture alternately with chocolate mixture and sour cream. Fold in egg white mixture. Pour about ⅓ of the batter into pan. Spoon over the coconut mixture; repeat until all batter and coconut mixture has been used up. Bake about 1 hour or until tester inserted in center comes out clean. Cool about 30 minutes. Invert onto plate and remove from pan. Frost with frosting of choice.

CHOCOLATE PRUNE CAKE

Makes one 5 × 9-inch loaf cake

½ **cup cocoa**
2 **cups sugar**
2 **cups flour, sifted**
1 **teaspoon baking soda**
1 **teaspoon baking powder**
2 **teaspoons cinnamon**
1 **teaspoon allspice**

3 **eggs**
¾ **cup butter**
1 **cup prunes, pitted, cooked,**
   chopped (juice reserved)
   Chocolate Icing for Prune Cake
   (see following recipe)

Preheat oven to 350°. Generously grease and lightly flour one 9 × 5 × 3-inch loaf pan. Sift together all dry ingredients. Mix dry ingredients with all remaining ingredients except icing, stirring well. If batter seems thick, add some prune juice. Pour batter into pan. Bake until tester inserted in center of cake comes out clean, 45 to 60 minutes. Cool in pan 20 minutes; complete cooling on wire rack. Frost with Chocolate Icing for Prune Cake.

CHOCOLATE ICING FOR PRUNE CAKE

Makes 1½ cups

1¼ **cups powdered sugar, sifted**
3 **heaping tablespoons cocoa**
2 **tablespoons butter**

1 **tablespoon hot milk**
1 **teaspoon vanilla extract**

Mix first 4 ingredients in a small saucepan until smooth; add vanilla. Bring to a boil, stirring constantly.

DATE CHOCOLATE CAKE

Makes one single-layer, 9 × 13-inch cake

1¼ cups dates, finely chopped
1 teaspoon baking soda
1 cup boiling water
1¾ cups flour, sifted
½ teaspoon salt
½ cup butter, softened
1 cup sugar
2 eggs

1 teaspoon vanilla extract
1 tablespoon orange peel, finely grated
6 ounces (1 cup) semisweet chocolate chips
½ cup nuts, finely chopped
Powdered sugar

Preheat oven to 350°. Grease and lightly flour a 9 × 13 × 2-inch pan. Mix together dates, baking soda and boiling water; set aside. Sift together flour and salt. Mix butter and sugar; beat until creamy. Add eggs, vanilla and orange peel, beating until well blended. Add flour mixture alternately with date mixture. Stir in ½ of chocolate chips. Pour into pan. Sprinkle with remaining chocolate chips and nuts. Bake until tester inserted in center comes out clean, 35 to 45 minutes. Cool in pan 5 minutes; complete cooling on wire rack. Serve with sifted powdered sugar on top.

OLD-FASHIONED COCOA CAKE

A favorite, spiked with peppermint.
Makes one 2-layer, 9-inch cake

⅔ cup butter
1⅔ cups sugar
3 eggs
⅔ cup cocoa
2¼ cups flour, sifted
1¼ teaspoons baking soda
¼ teaspoon baking powder

1 teaspoon salt
½ cup peppermint candy, finely crushed
½ cup water
1 teaspoon peppermint extract
Frosting of choice

Preheat oven to 350°. Grease two 9-inch cake pans and dust with cocoa. Cream butter, sugar and eggs until light and fluffy at high speed of mixer, 4 to 5 minutes. Sift together dry ingredients. Add to creamed mixture alternately with peppermint candy, water and peppermint extract. Continue beating at medium speed until batter and candy are well blended, 4 to 5 minutes. Pour into pans. Bake until tester inserted in center of cake comes out clean, about 30 minutes. Cool in pans 5 minutes; complete cooling on wire racks. Frost with frosting of choice.

WALNUT MERINGUE
CHOCOLATE CREAM CAKE

An elegant dessert—and so light!
Makes one 2-layer, 8-inch cake

2 cups sugar
½ cup butter
4 eggs, separated
½ teaspoon vanilla extract
⅓ cup milk
1 teaspoon baking powder

1 cup flour, sifted
¼ teaspoon salt
1 cup walnuts, chopped
⅓ cup cocoa
1½ cups whipping cream, whipped

Preheat oven to 325°. Grease lightly two 8-inch springform pans. Beat butter with ½ cup sugar until light. Beat in egg yolks one at a time. Add vanilla, milk and dry ingredients, which have been sifted together. Place in bottom of pans. For filling, beat egg whites until stiff; fold in walnuts and 1 cup sugar. Spread filling over batter in pans. Bake 60 minutes (layers will not be very high). Cool in pans 5 minutes; complete cooling on wire racks. For icing, mix cocoa and remaining ½ cup sugar; fold carefully into whipped cream. Spread icing on one layer, top with other and carefully spread icing over tops and sides.

HAWAIIAN CHOCOLATE
PINEAPPLE CAKE

A tropical delight.
Makes one single-layer, 10 × 15-inch cake

½ cup coconut, flaked
¾ cup crushed pineapple,
    undrained
1 cup flour, sifted
¼ teaspoon baking soda
⅛ teaspoon salt
½ teaspoon baking powder

¼ cup butter
½ cup sugar
1/16 teaspoon ginger
1 egg
3 ounces (½ cup) semisweet
    chocolate chips

Preheat oven to 375°. Grease a 10 × 15 × 1-inch pan. Combine coconut and ¼ cup pineapple; set aside for topping. Sift together first four dry ingredients. Combine butter, sugar and ginger. Add egg; beat well. Blend in flour mixture and remaining pineapple. Add chocolate chips. Pour into pan; spread topping of coconut and pineapple evenly over top. Bake until tester inserted in center comes out clean, about 25 minutes.

SWEET 'N' SPICY
DEVIL'S FOOD CAKE

A mix makes this quick and apple butter makes it memorable.
Makes one 2-layer, 9-inch cake

1 (18½ ounces) package devil's food
   cake mix
2 eggs
1 cup apple butter
1 cup water

½ cup walnuts, chopped
Devilish Chocolate Frosting (see
   following recipe)
12 walnut halves

Preheat oven to 350°. Grease and flour two 9-inch cake pans. In large bowl of electric mixer place cake mix, eggs, apple butter, water and nuts. Beat until well moistened; beat about 3 minutes more at medium speed. Pour batter into pans. Bake until tester inserted in center comes out clean (time varies with brand of cake mix). Cool 10 minutes; remove from pan. Cool thoroughly on wire racks. Frost with Devilish Chocolate Frosting. Garnish with walnut halves.

DEVILISH CHOCOLATE
FROSTING

Makes about 3½ cups

4 ounces (4 squares) unsweetened
   chocolate
½ cup whipping cream
1/16 teaspoon salt

½ teaspoon butter, melted
1 egg, well beaten
1 teaspoon vanilla extract
2½ cups powdered sugar

Melt chocolate over hot water in top of double boiler. Stir in whipping cream, salt and butter; mix well. Remove from heat; blend in egg and vanilla. Stir in powdered sugar; beat until correct consistency to spread.

CHOCOLATE FUDGE CAKE

Makes one 2-layer, 9-inch cake

¾ cup butter
1¾ cups brown sugar, firmly packed
4 eggs
8 ounces (8 squares) unsweetened
   chocolate
2¼ cups flour

1½ teaspoons baking soda
¼ teaspoon salt
1½ cups milk
2 teaspoons vanilla extract
Frosting of choice

Preheat oven to 350°. Grease two 9-inch cake pans well. Cream butter with sugar. Add 1 whole egg; beat well. Separate 3 eggs, reserving egg whites. Add egg yolks to creamed mixture one at a time, beating well after each addition. Melt chocolate over hot water; add to egg mixture. Sift together dry ingredients; add alternately with milk to mixture. Pour into pans; bake until tester inserted in center comes out clean, about 45 minutes. Cool 5 minutes before removing from pans; complete cooling on wire racks. Frost with frosting of choice.

YOGURT DEVIL'S FOOD CAKE

The yogurt flavor is complemented by the cream cheese frosting.
Makes one 2-layer, 9-inch cake

2 ounces (2 squares) unsweetened
　chocolate
2 eggs, separated
1½ cups sugar
1½ teaspoons baking soda
¾ teaspoon salt
1¾ cups flour

⅓ cup cooking oil
1 cup plain yogurt
⅓ cup milk
Chocolate Cream Cheese Frosting
　(see following recipe)

Preheat oven to 350°. Line with waxed paper, grease and flour two 9-inch cake pans. Melt chocolate; cool. Beat egg whites until frothy. Gradually add ½ cup sugar, beating constantly until stiff and glossy; set aside. Sift together dry ingredients. Add cooking oil and about ½ cup yogurt; beat one minute. Add remaining yogurt, milk, egg yolks and chocolate; beat one minute more. Fold beaten egg whites into batter. Pour into pans. Bake until tester inserted in center of cake comes out clean, about 25 minutes. Cool on wire racks about 15 minutes. Remove from pans and cool completely. Frost with Chocolate Cream Cheese Frosting.

CHOCOLATE CREAM CHEESE FROSTING

Makes about 2½ cups

⅓ cup cream cheese, softened
3 tablespoons cocoa

1/16 teaspoon salt
2 cups powdered sugar

Mix all ingredients well until creamy.

RUM DEVIL'S FOOD CAKE

Easy, moist and subtly rum flavored.
Makes one 2-layer, 9-inch cake

1 (18.25 ounces) package devil's
    food cake mix
1 (3¼ ounces) package chocolate
    pudding and pie filling mix
1½ cups milk
⅓ cup rum

2½ cups whipping cream
½ cup powdered sugar
    Whipped cream, sweetened
      to taste
    Chocolate curls (optional)

Preheat oven to 350°. Grease two 9-inch cake pans. Prepare devil's food cake according to directions on package. Pour into pans. Bake until cake tester inserted in center of cake comes out clean. Cool in pans on wire rack 10 minutes. Turn layers out onto rack; cool completely. Prepare pudding-pie filling mix according to directions on package, using only 1½ cups milk instead of 2 cups called for. Bring to boil; remove from heat. Stir in all but 2 tablespoons of rum. Place in bowl, cover top with waxed paper. Refrigerate until chilled, about 2 hours. Beat ½ the whipping cream until stiff; fold into chilled custard. Beat remaining 2 cups of whipping cream with powdered sugar until stiff; fold in remaining rum. Refrigerate until needed. About an hour before serving, split each layer in half, making a total of 4 layers. Place one layer, with cut side up on plate. Spread evenly with ¾ cup custard filling; repeat this with two more layers and remaining filling. Place remaining layer, cut side down, on top. Frost sides and top with sweetened whipped cream. If desired decorate with chocolate curls. Return to refrigerator for an hour before serving.

■

FUDGE PUDDIN' CAKE

Makes one single-layer, 8 × 8-inch cake

1 cup flour, sifted
½ teaspoon salt
½ cup sugar
2 teaspoons baking powder
¾ cup nuts, chopped fine
½ cup milk
1 teaspoon vanilla extract

2 tablespoons butter, melted
1 ounce (1 square) unsweetened
    chocolate, melted
¼ cup cocoa
¾ cup brown sugar, firmly packed
1¾ cups hot water

Preheat oven to 375°. Grease an 8-inch square baking pan. Sift together dry ingredients; add nuts. Stir in milk, vanilla, butter and chocolate. Spread into pan. Mix cocoa, brown sugar and hot water; pour over batter. Bake 45 minutes. As pudding bakes, the batter rises through the sauce. Serve hot or cold.

JOSEPHINE'S FUDGE CAKE

My daughter-in-law's favorite fudge cake.
Makes one 10-inch Bundt cake

1½ cups unsalted butter
6 eggs
1½ cups sugar
2 cups flour
1 (14.5 ounces) package fudge
    frosting mix

2 cups nuts, chopped
½ teaspoon vanilla extract
½ teaspoon black walnut flavoring

Preheat oven to 350°. Thoroughly grease a 10-inch Bundt pan. Cream butter; add eggs one at a time, beating well after each addition. Gradually add sugar and continue to cream until very light and fluffy. Add flour, frosting mix, vanilla, black walnut flavoring and nuts, stirring by hand until well blended. Pour batter into pan. Bake until tester inserted in center of cake comes out clean, about 60 minutes. Cool 2 to 3 hours before removing from pan, then cool until ready to serve.

CHOCOLATE BUNDT CAKE

Rippled with cinnamon and flavored with sherry.
Makes one 10-inch Bundt cake

1 (18.25 ounces) package chocolate
    cake mix
1 (4.5 ounces) package instant
    chocolate pudding mix
¾ cup butter-flavored cooking oil
¾ cup sherry
4 eggs
1 tablespoon butter flavoring

1 teaspoon vanilla extract
¼ cup sugar
2 teaspoons cinnamon
½ teaspoon allspice
½ cup nuts, chopped
    Frosting of choice

Preheat oven to 350°. Grease well a 10-inch Bundt pan, but do not flour. Mix first seven ingredients together; beat 7 to 8 minutes at medium speed of mixer. Mix last four ingredients together. Put ½ of the cinnamon mixture in the cake pan; pour in half the cake batter. Add remaining cinnamon mixture, then remaining cake batter. Bake until cake tester inserted in center of cake comes out clean, about 45 minutes. Allow to cool in pan 10 minutes; remove from pan. Frost with frosting of choice.

CHOCOLATE ALMOND CAKE

Makes one 2-layer, 8-inch cake

½ cup butter
1¼ cups sugar
2 eggs
8 ounces (8 squares) unsweetened
   chocolate
1¾ cups flour
1 teaspoon baking soda

1/16 teaspoon salt
1 cup milk
1 teaspoon vanilla extract
   Boiled icing of choice
½ cup almonds, chopped

Preheat oven to 375°. Grease two 8-inch cake pans. Cream butter with sugar; add eggs, one at a time, beating well after each addition. Melt chocolate over hot water; add to creamed mixture. Sift together dry ingredients; add, alternating with milk, to creamed mixture. Add vanilla. Pour into pans. Bake until tester inserted in center comes out clean, about 30 minutes. Cool 5 minutes before removing from pans; then cool layers on a wire rack. When cool, spread boiled icing of choice between layers, which have been sprinkled with almonds. Spread remaining frosting on tops and sides of cake; garnish with almonds.

ITALIAN CHOCOLATE AND ALMOND CAKE

Parozzo, its Italian name, is an Italian friend's recipe.
Makes one 2-layer, 9-inch cake

½ cup flour, unsifted
⅓ cup potato flour
1½ teaspoons cinnamon
¼ teaspoon ground cloves
5 eggs, separated, at room
   temperature
¾ cup sugar

1 cup almonds, ground
⅓ cup unsweetened cocoa
5 tablespoons margarine, melted
   and cooled
2 teaspoons vanilla extract
   Chocolate filling of choice

Preheat oven to 350°. Grease and flour two 9-inch round cake pans. Mix dry ingredients. Beat egg whites until stiff but not dry. Beat egg yolks with sugar at highest speed of mixer until thick and lemon colored, 5 to 6 minutes. Add almonds and cocoa; mix well. Gradually add flour mixture, beating well after each addition. Add margarine and vanilla. Beat in well. Fold in egg whites. Pour into pans. Bake until cake tester inserted into center of cake comes out clean, 35 to 40 minutes. Cool in pans 10 minutes. Cool completely on wire racks. Spread layers with filling of choice. Layers will be thin.

CHOCOLATE
ALMOND POUND CAKE

Makes one 10-inch tube cake

1 cup unblanched almonds, sliced	4 eggs
¾ cup unsalted butter	¼ teaspoon almond extract
1 (18.25 ounces) package chocolate	½ cup water
cake mix	¼ cup powdered sugar, sifted

Preheat oven to 350°. Have ready a 10-inch tube pan which has been heavily buttered and sprinkled with ½ cup sliced almonds. Melt butter in saucepan and add remaining almonds; stir over medium heat until almonds are toasted and browned. Remove from heat; cool. Combine cake mix, eggs, almond extract, water and butter-almond mixture. Mix until all are well moistened; beat 5 minutes on medium speed of mixer. Pour batter into tube pan. Bake until tester inserted in center comes out clean, 45 to 50 minutes. Cool in pan about 10 minutes. Place on wire rack and cool completely. Sprinkle with powdered sugar.

SPANISH MARBLE CAKE

Makes one single-layer, 8 × 8-inch cake

1¾ cups flour, sifted	1 cup sugar
½ teaspoon salt	2 eggs, well beaten
2 teaspoons baking powder	1 teaspoon vanilla extract
1 ounce (1 square) unsweetened	½ cup plus 2 tablespoons milk
chocolate	Frosting of choice
½ cup butter	

Preheat oven to 350°. Grease and flour well an 8-inch square cake pan. Sift together first three ingredients. Melt chocolate over hot water. Cream butter. Gradually add sugar, continuing to beat until fluffy. Add eggs and vanilla; beat well. Add sifted dry ingredients alternately with ½ cup milk to egg mixture a little at a time. Divide batter into two parts. Combine chocolate and remaining milk; stir into one part of batter, blending well. Drop alternating spoonfuls of light and dark batters into cake pan. Bake until cake springs back when lightly touched with finger, about 45 minutes. Cool in pan a few minutes; remove. Cool completely on wire rack. Frost with frosting of choice.

GLAZED
CHOCOLATE CHIP POUND CAKE

Makes one 9 × 5-inch loaf cake

2¼ cups flour, sifted
2 teaspoons baking powder
1 cup sugar
1 teaspoon salt
½ cup butter
1 teaspoon vanilla extract
½ teaspoon black walnut flavoring

5 egg yolks
¾ cup milk
2 ounces (2 squares) unsweetened
    chocolate, grated
1 cup nuts, chopped
Fast Lemon Glaze
    (see following recipe)

Preheat oven to 350°. Grease and flour a 9 × 5 × 3-inch loaf pan. Sift together dry ingredients; add butter, vanilla, black walnut flavoring, egg yolks and ½ cup milk. Beat 2 minutes. Add remaining milk; beat another 2 to 3 minutes. Fold chocolate and nuts into batter; pour mixture into pan. Bake until tester inserted in center of cake comes out clean, 60 to 70 minutes. Pierce warm cake with fork. Pour Fast Lemon Glaze over top.

FAST LEMON GLAZE

Makes about ¾ cup

½ cup lemon juice   1 cup powdered sugar

Cook lemon juice and powdered sugar over low heat until powdered sugar is dissolved.

CHOCOLATE-GLAZED
POUND CAKE

A classic pound cake, glazed with chocolate.
Makes one 10 × 5-inch loaf cake

2½ cups flour, sifted
1 teaspoon salt
1 teaspoon baking soda
⅔ cup butter, softened
1 cup sugar

3 eggs
⅔ cup buttermilk
1 teaspoon vanilla extract
½ cup nuts, chopped
Chocolate Glaze

Preheat oven to 350°. Grease a 5 × 9 × 3-inch loaf pan. Melt chocolate over hot, not boiling, water; remove from heat and cool. Sift together flour, salt and soda. Combine butter and sugar; beat until creamy. Blend in cooled chocolate. Beat in eggs one at a time.

Stir in flour mixture, alternating with buttermilk. Add vanilla and chopped nuts and mix well. Pour into pan. Bake until tester inserted in center comes out clean, about 70 minutes. Cool in pan 15 minutes; complete cooling on wire rack. Spread top and sides with Chocolate Glaze.

CHOCOLATE GLAZE

Makes about 1½ cups

2 tablespoons butter
3 tablespoons water
¼ cup light corn syrup

6 ounces (1 cup) semisweet
chocolate chips

Combine first three ingredients. Bring to boil over moderate heat, stirring constantly; remove from heat. Stir in chocolate chips until smooth. Cool several minutes until thick enough to spread.

FUDGE CAKE SURPRISE

It may sound odd, but it's delicious!
Makes one 2-layer, 8-inch cake

⅔ cup butter
1½ cups sugar
3 eggs
1 teaspoon almond extract
1 cup beer
½ cup unsweetened cocoa
1 teaspoon baking powder

1 teaspoon salt
1 teaspoon baking soda
2¼ cups flour, sifted
⅔ cup sauerkraut, drained and
  chopped
Mocha Whipped Cream (see
  following recipe)

Preheat oven to 350°. Grease well and flour two 8-inch round or square cake pans. Cream butter with sugar; beat in eggs and almond extract. Add dry ingredients, which have been sifted together, alternately with beer. Stir in sauerkraut. Pour into pans. Bake until tester inserted in center of cake comes out clean. Cool in pans for 20 minutes; complete cooling on wire racks. Frost with Mocha Whipped Cream.

MOCHA WHIPPED CREAM

Makes 1¾ cups

1½ cups whipping cream
3 tablespoons sugar

1 tablespoon unsweetened cocoa
1 tablespoon instant coffee

Whip cream. Add remaining ingredients, beating until mixture forms soft peaks.

MARY'S CHOCOLATE CAKE

An impressive, quick and easy marble cake.
Makes one 2-layer, 8- or 9-inch cake

2 (3¼ ounces) packages chocolate
   pudding mix
2 tablespoons sugar
½ cup butter
2 eggs
1 cup flour
½ teaspoon salt

½ teaspoon baking soda
1 teaspoon cream of tartar
1 cup milk
1 teaspoon vanilla extract
   Frosting of choice

Preheat oven to 325°. Grease well two 8- or 9-inch cake pans. Combine chocolate pudding, sugar, butter and eggs; beat well. Sift together dry ingredients. Add alternately with milk to pudding mixture. Stir in vanilla. Pour into pans. Bake until tester inserted in center comes out clean, about 60 minutes. Cool in pans 20 minutes; complete cooling on wire racks. Frost and fill with frosting of choice.

RICH CHOCOLATE SPONGE CAKE

A richer sponge than Helen's.
Makes one 2-layer, 8- or 9-inch cake

6 eggs, separated
1¼ cups sugar
4 ounces (4 squares) unsweetened
   chocolate, melted
1 cup milk
1 cup flour

1 teaspoon baking powder
½ teaspoon vanilla extract
½ teaspoon black walnut flavoring
½ tablespoon butter
2⅔ tablespoons cocoa

Preheat oven to 350°. Grease two 8- or 9-inch cake pans. Beat egg yolks and sugar together. Blend in melted chocolate. Boil milk; add to mixture. Add sifted flour and baking powder; mix well. Add vanilla and black walnut flavoring. Beat 4 egg whites until stiff, reserving 2 egg whites for icing; fold in gently. Pour into pans. Bake until tester inserted in center of cake comes out clean, 20 to 25 minutes. Cool. For frosting, mix remaining egg whites, butter and cocoa. Spread between layers, over sides and top.

HELEN'S CHOCOLATE SPONGE

Makes four 4-inch cakes

4 ounces sweet chocolate
3 tablespoons butter
⅓ cup sugar
1/16 teaspoon salt

½ teaspoon vanilla extract
2 egg whites
½ cup whipping cream, whipped

Preheat oven to 375°. Lightly grease four custard cups with oil. Melt chocolate over hot water; remove from heat. Add butter and blend well. Add sugar, salt and vanilla; mix well. Beat egg whites until stiff. Stir chocolate mixture into egg whites gently, but completely. Fill custard cups. Set cups in a pan half filled with water. Carefully place in oven. Bake until table knife inserted in center of each comes out clean, 45 to 50 minutes. Garnish each with a dollop of whipped cream.

PAULA'S CHOCOLATE ANGEL FOOD CAKE

Makes one 9-inch angel food cake

¾ cup flour, sifted
½ cup cocoa
1 teaspoon cream of tartar
1¼ cups sugar
8 egg whites

1/16 teaspoon salt
1½ teaspoons vanilla extract
Paula's Chocolate Mocha Frosting
(see following recipe)

Preheat oven to 350°. Grease and flour a 9-inch angel food pan. Sift cocoa and flour together twice. Add cream of tartar and sugar. Beat egg whites with salt; fold in sugar and flour-cocoa mixture. Add vanilla. Pour into pan. Bake 15 minutes, then reduce heat to 300° and bake until tester comes out clean, about 45 minutes more. Cool on wire rack about 2 hours, then remove from pan with knife. Frost with Paula's Chocolate Mocha Frosting.

PAULA'S CHOCOLATE MOCHA FROSTING

1½ cups powdered sugar
½ cup cocoa
1 teaspoon vanilla extract

4 tablespoons butter, melted
3 tablespoons hot coffee, double strength

Sift sugar and cocoa. Add vanilla, butter and hot coffee. Beat until smooth. If too thick, thin with additional coffee. After frosting cake, allow frosting to harden.

SUPREME
CHOCOLATE CRUMB CAKE

Makes one single-layer, 10 × 15-inch cake

CAKE

  6 *ounces (1 cup) semisweet*
    chocolate chips
½ *cup butter*
  2 *cups flour, sifted*
  1 *teaspoon baking soda*
¾ *teaspoon salt*
  1 *cup brown sugar, firmly packed*
  1 *teaspoon vanilla extract*

  2 *eggs*
  1 *cup buttermilk*

TOPPING

½ *cup brown sugar, firmly packed*
¼ *cup butter, softened*
½ *teaspoon nutmeg*
¾ *cup flour, sifted*
½ *cup nuts, chopped*

Preheat oven to 350°. Grease a 10 × 15 × 1-inch pan. Melt chocolate chips and butter; remove from heat. Sift together flour, soda and salt; set aside. Stir brown sugar and vanilla into chocolate mixture. Add eggs, one at a time, beating well after each addition. Add flour mixture alternately with buttermilk. Pour into pan. For topping, combine brown sugar, butter and nutmeg. Add and mix in the flour until texture is crumbly; place this over mixture in pan. Sprinkle nuts over top. Bake about 25 minutes.

OLD-TIME
CHOCOLATE SPONGE CAKE

Makes one 2-layer, 8-inch cake

  4 *eggs, separated*
1½ *cups sugar*
  4 *ounces (4 squares) unsweetened*
    chocolate, melted
  1 *cup milk*

  1 *cup flour*
  3 *teaspoons baking powder*
  2 *teaspoons vanilla extract*
    Frosting of choice

Preheat oven to 375°. Generously grease two 8-inch cake pans. Beat egg yolks and sugar; blend in melted chocolate. Fold in flour and baking powder. Add vanilla. Beat egg whites until stiff. Fold into batter. Pour into pans. Bake until tester inserted in center of cake comes out clean, 20 to 25 minutes. Cool 10 minutes; remove from pans. Complete cooling on wire racks. Frost with frosting of choice.

OLD-FASHIONED
CHOCOLATE GINGERBREAD

Makes one single-layer, 8-inch square cake

½ cup butter
1 cup sugar
1 egg
4 tablespoons cocoa
½ teaspoon salt
1½ teaspoons baking soda
1 teaspoon allspice
½ teaspoon ginger

½ teaspoon cinnamon
½ teaspoon ground cloves
2½ cups flour, sifted
1 cup molasses
1 cup boiling water
Whipped cream (optional)

Preheat oven to 350°. Grease and flour an 8-inch square pan. Cream butter, sugar and egg together until light and fluffy; add dry ingredients, which have been sifted together. Combine molasses and hot water; add alternately with dry ingredients to creamed mixture. Pour into pan. Bake until tester inserted in center of cake comes out clean, 55 to 60 minutes. Cool 5 minutes; remove from pan. Serve warm or cold with whipped cream.

CHOCOLATE
MARSHMALLOW GINGERBREAD

Gingerbread filled and frosted with marshmallow and chocolate.
Makes one split-layer, 8-inch square cake

½ cup butter
¼ cup sugar
1 egg
½ cup dark molasses
1¾ cups flour
½ teaspoon ground cloves
½ teaspoon cinnamon
¼ teaspoon allspice

1 teaspoon baking soda
1 teaspoon ginger
½ teaspoon salt
½ cup milk
1 cup miniature marshmallows
4½ ounces (¾ cup) semisweet
  chocolate chips

Preheat oven to 350°. Grease an 8 × 8 × 2-inch pan. Cream butter and sugar. Add egg; beat well. Add molasses. Sift together dry ingredients; add alternately with milk to butter mixture, blending well. Pour into pan. Bake until tester inserted in center comes out clean, about 45 minutes; remove from oven. Cool. Split into two layers; fill and cover with marshmallows and chocolate chips. Return to oven until marshmallows are slightly melted.

CLASSIC CHOCOLATE ROLL

A stunning, grand dessert.
Makes one 15-inch wide roll

5 eggs, separated
1 teaspoon vanilla extract
4 teaspoons cocoa
1/16 teaspoon salt
1 cup powdered sugar sifted

Chocolate Roll Filling (see
  following recipe)
Chocolate Roll Frosting (see
  following recipe)

Preheat oven to 350°. Grease and line with waxed paper a 10 × 15-inch jelly-roll pan. Beat egg yolks; add vanilla. Beat egg whites with salt until stiff. Add sifted cocoa to egg yolks alternately with egg whites. Pour into pan; bake until cake tests done, 20 to 25 minutes. Turn out onto cloth or brown paper sprinkled with powdered sugar. Cover with slightly dampened cloth; cool. Transfer to serving platter; remove paper carefully. Spread with Chocolate Roll Filling, roll up and frost with Chocolate Roll Frosting. To serve cut with serrated knife.

CHOCOLATE ROLL FILLING

Makes about 1¼ cups

1 cup whipping cream
½ teaspoon vanilla extract
2 tablespoons powdered sugar,
  sifted

1 tablespoon Chocolate Frosting
(see following recipe)

Whip cream. Fold in powdered sugar, vanilla and 1 tablespoon frosting.

Variation: Substitute 1 teaspoon instant coffee for Chocolate Frosting or ¼ cup crushed peppermint candy for vanilla and sugar in filling.

CHOCOLATE ROLL FROSTING

Makes about 2 cups

2 cups powdered sugar
3 tablespoons cocoa
1 teaspoon vanilla extract

4 or more tablespoons coffee,
  double strength

Mix all ingredients. Beat until correct spreading consistency is reached, adding more coffee if necessary. Refrigerate until ready to use.

PISTACHIO CREAM CHOCOLATE ROLL

Makes one 8-inch roll

3 eggs, separated
6 tablespoons sugar
3 tablespoons cocoa
1 teaspoon vanilla extract
½ teaspoon almond extract

¼ teaspoon anise seed, finely ground
½ teaspoon cinnamon
    Cocoa Pistachio Whipped Cream Filling

Preheat oven to 350°. Line a well-greased 8-inch square cake pan with waxed paper; grease paper. Beat egg yolks until light and fluffy. Add sugar a tablespoon at a time, beating well after each addition until mixture is very creamy. Mix cocoa, vanilla and almond extracts, anise seed and cinnamon; stir into first mixture. Beat egg whites until stiff; gently fold into cocoa mixture. Pour into pan. Bake until cake shrinks from sides of pan, about 25 minutes. Cool 5 to 6 minutes. Remove cake from pan; remove waxed paper. Spread about ½ of the Cocoa Pistachio Whipped Cream Filling in middle of cooled cake; bring sides of cake together to form a roll. When ready to serve, cover roll with remaining whipped cream mix; sprinkle with pistachios. Cut into slices.

COCOA-PISTACHIO WHIPPED CREAM FILLING

Makes about 1¾ cups

2 tablespoons cocoa
1½ cups whipping cream
¼ cup sugar

½ teaspoon vanilla extract
2 tablespoons pistachio nuts, chopped and toasted

Mix all ingredients except nuts in a bowl. Place bowl in refrigerator several hours. Whip until mixture holds its shape (do not overwhip).

HASTY MARSHMALLOW CHOCOLATE CAKE

Makes one 2-layer, 8- or 9-inch cake

16 marshmallows
2 ounces (2 squares) unsweetened
  chocolate, grated
½ cup hot water
2 eggs
1 cup sugar
1 teaspoon vanilla extract

1½ cups flour, sifted
1 teaspoon baking soda
1 teaspoon salt
1 cup sour cream
  Frosting of choice

Preheat oven to 350°. Grease two 8- or 9-inch cake pans. Melt marshmallows and chocolate in hot water; set aside. Cream sugar and eggs; add vanilla and mix. Add sifted flour, soda and salt alternately with sour cream. Fold in marshmallow mixture last. Bake until tester inserted in center of cake comes out clean, 30 to 35 minutes. Cool in pans 5 minutes; complete cooling on wire racks. Frost with frosting of choice.

•

MARGARET'S FAMOUS CHOCOLATE NUT ROLL

My sister-in-law's very popular version.
Makes one 8-inch roll

CAKE
3 eggs, separated
6 tablespoons sugar
3 tablespoons cocoa
1 teaspoon black walnut flavoring
1 teaspoon vanilla extract
½ teaspoon allspice
¼ teaspoon cinnamon

FILLING
1½ cups whipping cream
4 tablespoons sugar
2 tablespoons cocoa
½ teaspoon almond extract
3 tablespoons pecans or almonds,
  very finely chopped

Preheat oven to 350°. Line a greased 8-inch square cake pan with waxed paper and grease paper. Beat egg yolks until very light and fluffy. Add sugar a tablespoon at a time, beating well after each addition (mixture will be very creamy). Stir in cocoa, flavorings and spices. Beat egg whites until stiff; gently fold into cocoa mixture. Pour into pan. Bake until cake shrinks from sides of pan, about 30 minutes. Cool a few minutes, then remove cake from pan. Peel off waxed paper. To prepare filling, in medium mixing bowl gently mix whipping cream, sugar, cocoa and almond extract. Chill bowl in refrigerator at least 4 hours, then whip mixture until it holds its shape. (Do not overwhip.) Place half the filling in center of cooled cake. Fold two sides of cake together so that they meet, forming a roll. Cover roll with remaining whipped cream mixture. Sprinkle with nuts; cut into slices.

■ ■

FREEZING CHOCOLATE CAKES

Chocolate cakes, like all baked goods, freeze beautifully. Freeze it now, frost it later; just be sure to wait until the cake has returned to room temperature before frosting it. The same is true for frozen cookies.

■ ■

COCONUT-FILLED
CHOCOLATE CAKE ROLL

Filled with crunchy nuts and coconut.
Makes one 10-inch roll

¼ cup unsalted butter	⅔ cup flour
1 cup nuts, finely chopped	¼ teaspoon salt
1⅓ cups coconut, flaked	¼ teaspoon baking powder
2 cups sweetened condensed milk	⅓ cup water
3 eggs	1 teaspoon black walnut flavoring
1 cup sugar	½ teaspoon vanilla extract
⅓ cup cocoa	1 cup powdered sugar

Preheat oven to 375°. Line a 10 × 15-inch jelly-roll pan with aluminum foil. Melt butter; pour over bottom of foil. Mix nuts and coconut together; sprinkle over butter in pan. Drizzle condensed milk over all. Beat eggs 2 minutes at high speed of mixer. Gradually add sugar, beating for another 2 to 3 minutes. Mix dry ingredients together; add to egg mixture. Stir in water, vanilla and black walnut flavoring. Blend 2 minutes at lowest speed of mixer. Pour into pan. Bake until tester inserted in center of cake comes out clean. Leaving cake in pan, sprinkle powdered sugar over top; cover with towel. Invert cake onto a large cookie sheet or very heavy aluminum foil placed under towel. Remove pan and aluminum foil. Starting with shortest side, roll up jelly-roll style, pushing with towel to roll. (Do not roll up towel in cake.) Keep wrapped in towel until ready to serve.

■

CHRISTMAS LOG

A traditional Christmas dessert in France.
Makes one 13-inch roll

5 eggs, separated
1 cup powdered sugar
3 tablespoons dark cocoa
½ teaspoon vanilla extract
6 tablespoons Chocolate-Coffee
   Butter Cream (see recipe, page
   99)

2 cups whipping cream
½ cup superfine sugar
¼ cup pistachio nuts, finely ground
   (garnish)
   Chocolate butter cream frosting
   of choice

Preheat oven to 350°. Grease well, line with waxed paper, grease again and flour a 9 × 13 × 2-inch pan. Beat egg yolks until thick and pale. Add sugar, cocoa and vanilla. Fold in egg whites, which have been beaten until stiff. Spread batter evenly in pan. Bake 12 to 15 minutes until tester inserted in center comes out clean. Loosen edges with sharp knife. Quickly turn cake onto a damp towel; sprinkle with powdered sugar. Trim edges. Roll cake in towel over rolling pin; cool. Unroll cake; spread it lightly with chocolate butter cream, and thickly with whipping cream whipped stiff with superfine sugar; roll up again. Spread chocolate butter cream frosting over roll using a spatula to roughen the surface to resemble bark. Decorate with swirls of frosting forced through a pastry bag; sprinkle ends of log with pistachio nuts.

Tortes

HUNGARIAN
CHOCOLATE POPPY SEED TORTE

Makes one 2-layer, 9-inch torte

½ cup poppy seeds
¼ cup butter, softened
½ cup sugar
6 eggs, separated
½ cup bread crumbs
4 ounces semisweet chocolate,
   melted

1 teaspoon cinnamon
   Raspberry jam
   Powdered sugar

Preheat oven to 325°. Grease and flour two 9-inch cake pans. Place poppy seeds in blender and blend until seeds are ground; set aside. Cream butter and sugar until light and fluffy; set aside. Beat egg yolks at medium speed of mixer until thick and lemon colored, about 5 to 6 minutes. Blend into butter mixture; add bread crumbs. Stir in chocolate, cinnamon and poppy seeds. Beat egg whites until stiff but not dry; fold into chocolate mixture. Pour into pans. Bake until cake tester inserted into center comes out clean, about 30 minutes. Immediately turn cakes onto wire racks to cool. When cool spread one layer with jam, cover with second layer and top with powdered sugar.

YUMMY CHOCOLATE COFFEE NUT TORTE

A tube cake, layered with rich coffee butter cream.
Makes one 9-inch tube torte

5 eggs, separated
1 cup sugar
1 tablespoon cocoa
1 teaspoon instant coffee

½ cup flour, sifted
½ cup nuts, finely ground
Chocolate-Coffee Butter Cream
(see following recipe)

Preheat oven to 325°. Grease and flour lightly a 9-inch tube pan. Beat egg whites until they form soft peaks. Gradually add sugar, beating until mixture stands in stiff peaks. Beat egg yolks until lemon colored and thick. Fold in cocoa, coffee, flour and nuts. Gently fold into egg whites until thoroughly mixed. Pour into pan. Bake until tester inserted in center comes out clean, about 60 minutes. Cool. Split cake into either two or four layers. Fill and frost with Chocolate-Coffee Butter Cream.

CHOCOLATE-COFFEE BUTTER CREAM

Makes about 3½ cups

⅔ cup unsalted butter, softened
2½ cups powdered sugar
1 tablespoon cocoa
2 tablespoons instant coffee

1 teaspoon vanilla extract
1 teaspoon black walnut flavoring
½ cup whipping cream

Cream butter and 2 cups of sugar until light and fluffy. Blend in cocoa, coffee, vanilla and black walnut flavoring. Add remaining sugar alternately with whipping cream. Beat until smooth. (Add additional cream if necessary for better spreading consistency.)

RUTH'S
VERY FAVORITE SACHERTORTE

One version of the famous Viennese torte.
Makes one single-layer, 8-inch torte

½ cup unsalted butter, softened
½ cup plus 6 tablespoons sugar
6 ounces (6 squares) semisweet
   chocolate, melted plus 1 square
   unmelted
4 egg yolks

½ cup plus 1 tablespoon flour,
   sifted
5 egg whites
½ teaspoon almond extract
2½ tablespoons raspberry jam
½ cup water

Preheat oven to 325°. Grease and flour lightly a deep 8-inch springform pan. Cream butter. Gradually add 6 tablespoons sugar; cream until fluffy. Add 6 ounces melted chocolate; blend thoroughly. Add egg yolks, one at a time, beating after each addition. Stir in flour. Beat egg whites until stiff but not dry; fold into batter. Add almond extract; blend well. Pour batter into pan. Bake on lowest shelf of oven until cake shrinks from sides of pan and springs back to touch, about 75 minutes. Remove from oven. Let cake stand 10 minutes on rack before turning out of pan. Turn cake out on rack, right side up, cooling completely. Place rack on waxed paper. Spread top of cake with raspberry jam. To make icing, combine remaining ½ cup sugar and water in a saucepan; simmer two minutes, stirring constantly. Remove from heat. Add remaining chocolate; stir until melted and smooth. Bring to a boil, stirring constantly. Remove from heat; stir until mixture starts to thicken. Pour over cake, letting icing run down sides.

■

CHOCOLATE CHIP COOKIE TORTE

Makes one 3-layer, 8-inch torte

⅔ cup butter
½ cup sugar
½ cup brown sugar, firmly packed
1 egg
1 teaspoon vanilla extract
½ teaspoon black walnut flavoring
1½ cups flour

½ teaspoon salt
½ teaspoon baking soda
½ cups nuts, chopped
6 ounces (1 cup) semisweet
   chocolate chips
½ cup light corn syrup
1½ cups whipping cream

Preheat oven to 375°. Line 3 baking sheets with aluminum foil. Mix thoroughly butter, sugars, egg, vanilla and black walnut flavoring. Blend in dry ingredients. Mix in nuts. Divide dough into 3 parts. Flour hands and pat each part into an 8-inch circle on baking sheet. Bake until lightly browned, 12 to 13 minutes. Cool. Stir chocolate chips and corn syrup in a saucepan over low heat until chocolate melts; set aside. Pour ¼ cup whipping cream over 1 circle. Beat remaining whipping cream until stiff; spread soaked cookie circle with ⅓ whipped cream. Place second cookie circle on top; cover with half the chocolate mixture and more whipped cream. Place last circle on top; spread with other half of chocolate mixture. Spread remaining whipped cream over top to decorate. Cover and chill overnight. Remove from refrigerator about 15 minutes before serving.

SURPRISE CHOCOLATE TORTE

Makes one single-layer, 9-inch torte

8 eggs, separated	2 cups whipping cream
1 teaspoon vanilla extract	3 tablespoons sugar
1¼ cups powdered sugar, sifted	1 tablespoon instant coffee
½ cup cocoa	Chocolate curls (garnish)
1/16 teaspoon salt	

Preheat oven to 325°. Grease a 9-inch springform pan. Beat egg yolks and vanilla until thick and lemon colored. Sift together powdered sugar and cocoa. Blend into beaten egg yolks; beat 2 minutes. Beat egg whites and salt until they stand in peaks. Carefully fold egg yolk mixture into egg whites. Pour into pan. Bake until tester inserted in center comes out clean, 45 to 50 minutes. Remove from oven. Cool on a rack (the center will fall). Gently loosen from sides of pan. Remove. Whip cream; add sugar and instant coffee. Continue to whip until very stiff. Spoon into center of torte; garnish with chocolate curls. Refrigerate 3 to 4 hours before serving.

SUPER-DUPER CHOCOLATE TORTE

A dense torte, flavored with sweet wine.
Makes one single-layer, 10-inch torte

6 ounces (1 cup) semisweet chocolate chips	6 eggs, separated
½ cup unsalted butter	¾ cup Muscatel wine
½ teaspoon salt	1½ cups almonds, ground
1 cup sugar	½ cup bread crumbs, finely crushed
	1 cup whipping cream, whipped

Preheat oven to 350°. Generously grease a 10-inch springform pan with butter; dust well with fine bread crumbs. Melt chocolate chips over hot water; cool. Mix butter, salt and sugar; beat until light and fluffy. Add egg yolks one at a time, beating well after each addition. Add melted chocolate; stir well. Add ½ cup wine, nuts and crumbs. Beat egg whites until stiff as possible; fold gently into chocolate mixture. Pour into pan. Bake about 60 minutes. Remove from oven; drizzle remaining wine over top while still warm. Cool. Cover tightly and store in refrigerator. Before serving, place a dollop of whipped cream on top of each slice.

CHOCOLATE ALMOND TORTE

Makes one 2-layer, 9-inch torte

¾ cup butter
¾ cup sugar
7 eggs, separated
1 teaspoon vanilla extract
4 ounces sweet chocolate, melted
   and cooled

1 cup unblanched almonds, finely
   ground
½ teaspoon baking powder
   Chocolate Nut Torte Filling (see
   following recipe)
¼ cup blanched almonds, chopped

Preheat oven to 350°. Generously grease two 9-inch cake pans. Cream sugar and butter; beat in egg yolks, one at a time. Add vanilla. Blend in melted chocolate. Gently fold in ground almonds mixed with baking powder. Fold in egg whites, which have been beaten until stiff. Pour mixture into pans. Bake until tester inserted into center comes out clean, about 30 minutes. Cool away from drafts. Frost between layers and top with Chocolate Nut Torte Filling. Sprinkle with chopped almonds.

CHOCOLATE NUT TORTE FILLING

Makes about 2½ cups

4 eggs, beaten slightly
½ teaspoon cornstarch
¼ cup sugar
1/16 teaspoon salt

4 ounces sweet chocolate, melted
½ cup butter, softened
½ cup walnuts, ground
1 teaspoon vanilla extract

Mix eggs, cornstarch, sugar and salt in top of double boiler. Heat over boiling water until mixture thickens, but does not boil; cool. Stir in melted chocolate. Beat in butter a tablespoon at a time. Fold in nuts and vanilla.

BOSILJKA
MARICH'S SERBIAN TORTE

A beautiful combination of lemon and chocolate.
Makes one 4-layer, 9-inch torte

10 eggs, separated
1¾ cups sugar
 ¼ cup dry bread crumbs
  1 teaspoon lemon peel, grated
 ¼ cup lemon juice
 ¼ teaspoon lemon extract
 ½ cup blanched almonds, very
      finely ground

3 ounces (3 squares) unsweetened
    chocolate, melted
½ cup butter, softened
1 teaspoon vanilla extract
¼ cup sliced almonds, toasted
    (garnish)

Preheat oven to 350°. Line bottoms of four 9-inch cake pans with unglazed brown paper. Beat whites until stiff. Gradually beat in 1 cup sugar. Fold in bread crumbs, lemon peel, juice and lemon extract. Fold in ground almonds. Divide mixture into pans. Bake until faintly brown, about 20 minutes. Cool in pans on wire racks; remove. Beat egg yolks lightly; place with remaining sugar in top of double boiler. Cook over hot water until sugar is dissolved and mixture thickens (do not boil as this will curdle mixture). Remove from heat. Beat in melted chocolate; gradually beat in butter. Place in refrigerator until mixture reaches spreading consistency. Fill and frost layers. Garnish with sliced almonds. Refrigerate until firm.

CHOCOLATE SPONGE TORTE

Makes one 3-layer, 9-inch torte

¾ cup flour, sifted
½ teaspoon baking powder
½ teaspoon salt
5 eggs
¾ cup plus 2 tablespoons sugar
2½ ounces (2 squares) unsweetened
      chocolate

¼ cup cold water
¼ teaspoon baking soda
3 tablespoons brandy
    Chocolate frosting of choice

Preheat oven to 350°. Line three 9-inch cake pans with waxed paper. Sift together dry ingredients. Beat eggs until thick and lemon colored. Beat in ¾ cup sugar a tablespoon at a time, beating well after each addition. Carefully blend in flour mixture with a rubber spatula; set aside. Melt chocolate in top of double boiler over hot water; remove from heat. Add cold water at once. Add baking soda, sugar and remaining 2 tablespoons sugar; stir until thick and smooth. Blend mixture into batter. Stir in 1 tablespoon brandy. Pour 2½ cups batter into each of two cake pans; place remaining batter in third pan. Bake about 10 minutes, then test last pan, which contains least amount of batter, with cake tester to see if it comes out clean. If so, remove pan; bake remaining pans a few minutes more until each tests done. Loosen cakes from edges of pans; remove at once. Cool on wire racks. Break flattest cake into small pieces and allow to dry out. Break into fine crumbs. Using remaining brandy, sprinkle over two remaining layers. Spread one layer with frosting of choice; top with other layer. Frost sides and top. Sprinkle dry crumbs over tops and sides of torte. Refrigerate until firm.

·

SHOKOLADNO-MINDALNY TORTE

See what a difference mashed potatoes can make.
Makes one single-layer, 8-inch torte

1 cup butter, softened
2 cups sugar
4 eggs, separated
1 cup potatoes, mashed, at room
   temperature
1 cup almonds, ground
4 ounces (4 squares) unsweetened
   chocolate, melted and cooled
½ cup milk
2 teaspoons vanilla extract

½ cup orange marmalade, melted
1½ cups cake flour
2 teaspoons baking powder
1 teaspoon cinnamon
¼ teaspoon nutmeg
⅛ teaspoon ground cloves
   Chocolate-Cinnamon Mocha
     Frosting (see following recipe)
   Blanched almonds, halved
   (optional)

Preheat oven to 325°. Grease well and flour an 8-inch springform pan. Cream butter and sugar until fluffy. Beat in egg yolks; mix well. Add mashed potatoes, almonds, chocolate, milk, marmalade and vanilla; mix well. Combine remaining dry ingredients, add to chocolate mixture and stir until completely mixed. Beat egg whites until stiff, but not dry; fold into batter. Pour into pan; smooth top with a spatula. Bake until cake tester inserted into the center of cake comes out clean, about 75 minutes. Place on rack. Cool for 10 minutes; remove sides of pan and cool to room temperature. Cut into two layers crosswise. Spread sides and top with Chocolate-Cinnamon Mocha Frosting. Garnish with blanched almond halves, if desired.

CHOCOLATE-CINNAMON
MOCHA FROSTING

Makes about 3½ cups

6 tablespoons butter, softened
3 cups powdered sugar
½ cup cold coffee, double strength
2 ounces (2 squares) unsweetened
   chocolate, melted and cooled

½ teaspoon cinnamon
2 teaspoons vanilla extract

Cream butter and powdered sugar, then beat in rest of ingredients. Place in refrigerator until firm enough to spread easily, 15 to 20 minutes.

Ice Box Cakes

MOCHA REFRIGERATOR CAKE

Makes one 2-layer, 9 × 13-inch cake

¾ cup semisweet chocolate chips
1 tablespoon instant coffee
3 eggs, separated
½ teaspoon vanilla extract

½ teaspoon almond extract
18 ladyfingers
1 cup whipping cream, whipped

Line a 9 × 13-inch pan with waxed paper. Separate ladyfingers. Melt chocolate and coffee in top of double boiler; cook over hot water until chocolate melts. Blend well; remove from heat. Add egg yolks one at a time, beating well after each addition. Beat egg whites until stiff. Mix in thoroughly, but carefully. Add vanilla and almond extracts. Place 12 ladyfinger halves in bottom of pan. Spread with ½ mocha filling. Add another layer of ladyfinger halves. Spread with remaining filling; top with ladyfingers. Chill 3 to 4 hours. Whip cream. Remove cake from pan. Frost with whipped cream.

MOCHA-NUT ICE BOX CAKE

Mocha again, but with nuts and marshmallows.
Makes one single-layer, 10-inch cake

2½ cups marshmallows
  1 cup coffee, double strength
  1 ounce (1 square) bitter chocolate
32 ladyfingers

3 cups whipping cream
¾ cup nuts, finely chopped
¼ teaspoon salt

Line sides of 10-inch springform pan with whole ladyfingers, and bottom with ladyfingers which have been split in half. Melt marshmallows, chocolate, salt and coffee in top of double boiler; cool. When cool add stiffly whipped cream and all but 2 tablespoons of nuts. Pour half the marshmallow mixture into pan. Cover with split ladyfingers. Add other half of marshmallow mixture. Sprinkle top with remaining nuts. Refrigerate overnight.

AIRY MOCHA-ORANGE CREAM CAKE

Makes one 3-layer loaf cake

2½ cups imitation cream dessert
    topping, whipped
  2 teaspoons sugar
½ teaspoon almond or vanilla
    extract

1 tablespoon cocoa
1 teaspoon instant coffee
1 orange chiffon loaf cake

Dessert topping must be stiff. Gradually add sugar and vanilla or almond extract. Divide into halves; stir cocoa and coffee into one half. Slice cake into three layers; spread mocha filling between layers. Use remaining whipped topping to frost sides and top of cake. Refrigerate overnight.

ALMOND CHOCOLATE ICE BOX CAKE

Makes 4 servings

1 cup whipping cream, whipped
½ cup chocolate-covered almonds,
    finely chopped

16 graham crackers
16 whole chocolate-covered almonds
    (garnish)

Add chopped almonds to ½ cup stiffly whipped cream. Spread on graham crackers and stack to form a loaf. Wrap in waxed paper; place in refrigerator at least 12 hours. Just before serving, spread remaining whipped cream on loaf. Garnish with whole almonds.

CHOCOLATE ICE BOX TORTE

A quick, make-ahead torte.
Makes one single-layer, 9-inch torte

4½ ounces (¾ cup) semisweet
    chocolate chips
2 tablespoons sugar
2½ tablespoons water
4 eggs, separated

1 teaspoon vanilla
30 chocolate wafers, crushed
1 cup whipping cream
3 tablespoons sugar

Combine chocolate chips, sugar and water in top of double boiler. Place over boiling water; heat until blended, stirring constantly. Remove from heat; cool. Add egg yolks one at a time, beating thoroughly after each addition. Add vanilla. Chill. Beat egg whites until stiff but not dry; fold in. Line a 9-inch pie plate with ½ the crushed cookies. Fill with chocolate mixture. Top with remaining crushed cookies. Refrigerate overnight. Serve with whipped cream, sweetened with sugar.

SIX-LAYER
CHOCOLATE ICE BOX LOAF CAKE

Makes one 6-layer, 9 × 5-inch loaf cake

3 ounces (½ cup) sweet chocolate
1 tablespoon water
1/16 teaspoon salt
2 egg yolks

½ teaspoon vanilla extract
1 cup whipping cream, whipped
1 loaf pound cake

Line bottom and sides of a 9 × 5 × 2-inch loaf pan with waxed paper, extending paper beyond rim of pan. Combine chocolate and water in saucepan over low heat, stirring until chocolate is melted. Add salt and egg yolks, one at a time, beating well after each addition. Add vanilla. Cool. Fold into whipped cream; chill. Cut loaf pound cake into six slices lengthwise; chill slightly. Spread chilled chocolate mixture between slices and on sides and top of cake. Refrigerate overnight.

CHOCOLATE IN THE SNOW

An elegant-looking dessert that can be made hours ahead.
Makes 8 servings

4 eggs
½ cup sugar
1 envelope (1 ounce) premelted
   unsweetened chocolate
or
1 square (1 ounce) unsweetened
   chocolate, melted and cooled

⅔ cup coconut macaroons, finely
   grated
2 cups whipping cream, whipped
   Ladyfingers
   Whipped cream (garnish)

Separate eggs, placing egg yolks in large bowl. Add sugar to egg yolks; beat until thick and lemon colored. Stir in chocolate; beat until well blended and very thick. Mix in grated macaroons; set mixture aside. Beat egg whites until they form stiff peaks. Gently fold beaten egg whites into chocolate mixture; fold in whipped cream. Line 8 individual dessert dishes (or 10-inch mold or large serving bowl) with ladyfingers. Spoon chocolate mixture over and place in refrigerator until firm. Garnish with additional whipped cream.

CHOCOLATE-PEPPERMINT
ICE BOX CAKE

Makes 10 to 12 servings

36 ladyfingers
 8 ounces sweet chocolate
 4 eggs, separated
 3 tablespoons sugar
 1 tablespoon water

1 teaspoon peppermint extract
1½ teaspoons vanilla extract
1 cup whipping cream
3 tablespoons powdered sugar

Line a 10-inch springform pan with ladyfingers, flat sides against rim of pan. Melt chocolate in top of double boiler. Beat egg yolks with sugar and water. Add to melted chocolate along with 1 teaspoon vanilla and peppermint extracts. Beat egg whites; fold in. Pour half of chocolate mixture into pan; place layer of ladyfingers on top. Add remaining chocolate mixture; top with remaining ladyfingers. Refrigerate overnight. Remove side of pan. Top with whipped cream flavored with powdered sugar and remaining vanilla.

Other Delights

CHOCOLATE MARSHMALLOW TEA CAKES

Makes 1½ dozen cupcakes

1¼ cups flour, sifted
2½ teaspoons baking powder
1/16 teaspoon salt
6 tablespoons cocoa
1/3 cup butter

¾ cup sugar
2 eggs, beaten
2/3 cup milk
18 miniature marshmallows

Preheat oven to 350°. Grease well three 6-cup muffin pans. Sift together first four ingredients three times. Cream butter with sugar; add eggs; beat until light. Add to flour mixture a little at a time, beating until smooth after each addition. Fill muffin pans and bake about 25 minutes or until tester inserted in center comes out clean. Just before removing from oven, place a marshmallow on each cupcake and allow to melt slightly.

BROWNIE-STYLE CUPCAKES

Dense, chocolaty cupcakes with bran.
Makes 1 dozen cupcakes

1 cup sugar
1 cup butter
2 eggs, beaten
2 ounces (2 squares) unsweetened
  chocolate

1/3 cup flour
½ teaspoon salt
½ cup bran
1 cup nuts, finely chopped
1 teaspoon vanilla extract

Preheat oven to 350°. Grease a 12-cup cupcake pan. Cream sugar and butter; add beaten eggs. Melt chocolate over hot water; add to mixture and beat thoroughly. Mix flour, salt, bran and nuts together; add to chocolate mixture. Add vanilla and mix well. Spread in pan; bake until tester inserted in a cake comes out clean, about 45 minutes. Cool in pan 20 minutes; remove.

CHOCOLATE WEARY WILLIES

Makes 1 dozen cupcakes

½ cup butter
1 ounce (1 square) unsweetened
   chocolate
1 cup sugar
1 cup flour
1 teaspoon baking powder

¼ teaspoon salt
2 eggs
½ cup milk
½ teaspoon vanilla extract
   Icing of choice (optional)

Preheat oven to 375°. Grease and flour two 6-cup muffin pans. Slowly melt butter and chocolate together. Sift together dry ingredients three times. Mix eggs with milk. Combine with flour mixture; add melted ingredients and vanilla. Beat thoroughly. Fill muffin pans; bake until tester inserted in a cake comes out clean, about 15 to 20 minutes. Cool. Ice if you wish.

CHOCOLATE CREAM DESSERT PANCAKES

Makes 6 pancakes

3 eggs, well beaten
½ cup milk
½ teaspoon almond extract
½ cup pancake mix
¼ cup sugar

1 cup whipping cream, whipped
2 teaspoons cocoa, sifted
1 teaspoon instant coffee
½ cup nuts, chopped

Combine eggs and milk. Add almond extract and pancake mix; stir until smooth. Place a teaspoon of butter in small frying pan; heat until butter bubbles. Pour in sufficient batter to coat bottom of pan with thin layer; cook until delicately browned on underside. Turn and bake on other side. Continue until all batter is used. Cool. Combine remaining ingredients. Place a small amount of cream mixture on edge of each pancake, and roll up jelly-roll style.

MOTHER'S CHOCOLATE WAFFLES

Serve these for brunch with fresh strawberries.
Makes 8 waffles

2 cups flour
3 teaspoons baking powder
¼ cup cocoa
¼ teaspoon salt
4 tablespoons sugar
2 eggs, separated

1½ cups milk
6 tablespoons butter, melted
1 cup whipping cream, whipped
  (optional)
1 cup hot chocolate syrup
  (optional)

Sift together dry ingredients. Beat egg yolks; add milk. Combine with dry ingredients. Mix until smooth; add butter. Beat egg whites until stiff; fold into mixture. Cook according to directions for operating waffle iron. Serve piping hot. For dessert waffles, top with hot chocolate syrup and dollop of whipped cream.

■

CHOCOLATE GLAZED DOUGHNUTS

Makes 20 doughnuts

4 ounces (4 squares) unsweetened
  chocolate
4 tablespoons butter
2 eggs
1½ cups sugar
½ teaspoon salt
4 teaspoons baking powder
4 cups flour

1 cup milk
Cooking oil or shortening for
  frying
2 cups powdered sugar, sifted
5 tablespoons boiling water
¼ cup coconut, finely grated
  Coconut (optional)

Melt ¼ of the chocolate with 1 tablespoon butter over hot water; cool. Beat eggs and sugar until blended; add cooled chocolate mixture. Sift together dry ingredients; add alternately with milk to egg mixture. On a floured board roll out dough about ⅓-inch thick. Cut with floured doughnut cutter. Fry 3 to 4 minutes in oil or shortening, which has been heated to 375°. Drain on paper towels. For glaze, melt remaining chocolate with remaining butter over hot water; stir in powdered sugar and enough boiling water to make thin glaze. Dip doughnuts into glaze and place on wire rack. Sprinkle with coconut if desired. These may be frozen.

■

CHAPTER FOUR

FROSTINGS, FILLINGS AND GLAZES

Frostings

SILKY CHOCOLATE FROSTING

Frosts one 2-layer, 9-inch cake

6 tablespoons sugar
6 tablespoons flour
2 cups milk
1 cup butter

1 teaspoon vanilla or almond
  extract
2 ounces (2 squares) unsweetened
  chocolate, melted

Mix sugar and flour; add milk slowly. Stir until smooth. Cook over low heat until thick, stirring constantly. Add butter, vanilla or almond extract and chocolate. Stir well; cool.

UNCOOKED CHOCOLATE ICING

Quick and easy.
Frosts one single-layer, 8-inch cake

1 tablespoon butter
1 ounce (1 square) unsweetened
  chocolate

1 cup powdered sugar, sifted
2 tablespoons half-and-half
½ teaspoon vanilla extract

Mix all ingredients together. Add more half-and-half if needed for spreading consistency.

CHOCOLATE BUTTER ICING

Frosts one 2-layer, 9-inch cake

3 cups powdered sugar
⅓ cup butter
3 tablespoons whipping cream

3 ounces (3 squares) unsweetened
  chocolate

Sift sugar, soften butter and melt chocolate. Beat all ingredients together until fluffy.

FAST CHOCOLATE FROSTING

Quick and rich.
Frosts one 2-layer, 9-inch cake

2 tablespoons butter, browned
1½ cups powdered sugar
2 heaping tablespoons cocoa

1 teaspoon vanilla or almond
  extract
¼ cup whipping cream

Mix first four ingredients; add whipping cream to reach spreading consistency.

CREAMY WALNUT CHOCOLATE FROSTING

Frosts 1½ dozen cupcakes

6 ounces (1 cup) semisweet
  chocolate chips
½ cup evaporated milk
3 cups powdered sugar

½ teaspoon black walnut flavoring
1/16 teaspoon salt
¼ cup butter, softened

Melt chocolate chips over hot water. Combine evaporated milk, sugar, black walnut flavoring and salt. Add chocolate. Beat until well blended. Add butter, beating until mixture is sufficiently thick to spread (let frosting stand about 20 minutes until thicker). Use immediately. If too thick, add a little additional milk.

MARY'S BUTTER FROSTING

Butterscotch gives this a wonderful, buttery flavor.
Frosts one 2-layer, 9-inch cake

6 ounces (1 cup) semisweet
  chocolate chips
1/3 cup butterscotch chips

½ cup evaporated milk
1/16 teaspoon salt

Stir chocolate and butterscotch chips over hot water until smooth. Bring evaporated milk and salt to a boil, stirring constantly; stir into melted chocolate mixture. Cool until sufficiently thick to spread.

CHOCOLATE RUM
FILLING AND FROSTING

Frosts one 2-layer, 9-inch cake

¾ cup sugar
1½ tablespoon arrowroot
1 cup milk
2 ounces (2 squares) unsweetened chocolate

4 egg yolks, lightly beaten
1 teaspoon rum flavoring
¼ cup butter, softened

Combine sugar and arrowroot in saucepan; gradually stir in milk, making a smooth paste. Add chocolate. Cook over medium heat, stirring constantly until thick and smooth, 5 to 6 minutes. Remove from heat; beat a few minutes. Stir a small amount of hot chocolate mixture into egg yolks; blend well. Add this to rest of chocolate mixture; continue to cook over low heat, stirring constantly for another minute. Add rum flavoring and chill. Cream butter until fluffy. Add chilled chocolate mixture to butter; beat until filling is smooth.

PAULA'S
CHOCOLATE CREAM FROSTING

A thicker chocolate frosting.
Frosts one single-layer 10 × 15-inch cake or 1½ dozen cupcakes

¼ cup cocoa mix
¼ cup brown sugar, firmly packed

1 cup whipping cream, chilled

Mix all ingredients together until sufficiently thick to hold shape. Use to frost cakes or cupcakes. Chill in refrigerator before serving.

SIMPLE FROSTING

Frosts one 2-layer, 8- or 9-inch cake

1¼ cups sweetened condensed milk
¼ teaspoon salt
¼ cup butter

6 ounces (1 cup) semisweet chocolate chips
1 teaspoon vanilla extract

Bring first three ingredients to boil over moderate heat, stirring constantly. Remove from heat; stir in chocolate chips until smooth. Add vanilla. Cool until thick enough to spread.

OLD-FASHIONED CHOCOLATE FROSTING

Great for frosting cakes, cupcakes or cookies.
Frosts one single-layer, 8-inch cake

1 tablespoon butter
1 ounce (1 square) unsweetened chocolate

3 tablespoons whipping cream
1½ cups powdered sugar, sifted

Melt butter and chocolate together in top of double boiler, being careful not to scorch. Blend in whipping cream and sugar; stir until very smooth.

·

FESTIVE CHOCOLATE TOPPING

Sweetened with honey and filled with candied fruit and coconut.
Frosts one 2-layer, 9-inch cake

2 tablespoons butter
¼ teaspoon salt
2 tablespoons cocoa
½ cup honey

2 tablespoons whipping cream
½ cup nuts, chopped
½ cup candied fruit, chopped
½ cup coconut, shredded

Mix butter, salt, cocoa and honey with whipping cream in a small bowl. Add nuts, fruit and coconut; mix well. After spreading on cake, place under broiler until topping bubbles and nuts brown lightly, 3 to 5 minutes.

·

CHOCOLATE BANANA COATING

A delicious coating for graham crackers and cookies.
Makes 4 cups

3 bananas, well mashed
½ cup peanut butter
¹⁄₁₆ teaspoon salt

½ teaspoon vanilla extract
6 ounces (1 cup) semisweet chocolate chips, melted

Blend bananas with peanut butter, salt and vanilla. Stir into melted chocolate chips.

·

CHOCOLATE MARBLEIZED
LOUISIANA FROSTING

Frosts one 2-layer, 9-inch cake

6 ounces (1 cup) semisweet
  chocolate chips
1 tablespoon water

3 tablespoons light corn syrup
1 (14.5 ounces) package white
  frosting mix

Mix first three ingredients well, stirring over low heat until smooth; remove from heat. Make frosting mix according to package directions; add chocolate mixture. Fold in with spatula; do not mix.

CHOCOLATE HONEY FROSTING

Honey flavored with a hint of coffee.
Frosts one 2- or 3-layer, 8-inch cake

3 ounces (½ cup) semisweet
  chocolate chips
1 tablespoon water
2 tablespoons honey

1½ cups whipping cream
⅛ teaspoon salt
¼ teaspoon instant coffee

Mix chocolate chips, water and honey over low heat until well blended; remove from heat. Cool until thick. Beat whipping cream, adding salt and coffee. Gently fold in chocolate mixture until well blended.

NUTTY CHOCOLATE FROSTING

Flavored with maple.
Frosts one 2-layer, 9-inch cake

1½ cups powdered sugar
½ cup butter
  2 ounces (2 squares) unsweetened
    chocolate, melted
1 egg

¼ teaspoon salt
1 teaspoon vanilla extract
½ teaspoon maple flavoring
1 cup nuts, chopped

Cream sugar and butter. Add melted chocolate, egg and remaining ingredients. Blend until smooth.

CHOCOLATE CAKE DECORATION TIP

Impress your guests with professional-looking chocolate decorations on any plain frosted cake. Place a strip of waxed paper on a cookie sheet. Melt sweet chocolate over hot water. Spread the melted chocolate carefully into 1-inch rounds on the waxed paper. Chill them in the refrigerator until the chocolate hardens. With cool hands, peel the rounds from the waxed paper and quickly press them into the frosting on the cake in any design you wish.

CHOCOLATE-NUT BOILED ICING

Frosts one single-layer, 9-inch cake

1 cup sugar
½ cup water
⅛ teaspoon cream of tartar
1 ounce (1 square) unsweetened chocolate, melted

2 egg whites, beaten stiff
½ teaspoon vanilla extract
½ cup nuts, chopped

Combine sugar, water, chocolate and cream of tartar; boil until mixture spins a thread when dropped from a spoon or reaches 230° on candy thermometer. Pour slowly over beaten egg whites, beating constantly until thick and cool enough to spread. Add vanilla and nuts.

RUTH'S QUICK CHOCOLATE FROSTING

Chopped almonds add texture to this frosting.
Frosts one 2-layer, 8-inch cake

2 ounces (2 squares) unsweetened chocolate
1⅓ cups sweetened condensed milk

1 tablespoon water
1 teaspoon almond extract
½ cup blanched almonds, chopped

Cook chocolate and milk in top of double boiler, stirring until chocolate melts and mixture thickens. Stir until well blended. Add water and almond extract; cool. Spread on cake. Sprinkle with almonds.

YUMMY CHOCOLATE ICING

Frosts one 2-layer, 9-inch cake

2 ounces (2 squares) unsweetened
  chocolate, finely chopped
1½ cups sugar
7 tablespoons milk
2 tablespoons butter

2 tablespoons vegetable shortening
1 tablespoon corn syrup
¼ teaspoon salt
1 teaspoon vanilla extract
½ cup nuts, finely chopped

Combine first seven ingredients; bring mixture slowly to full boil. Boil 1 minute, stirring constantly. Cool to lukewarm; add vanilla. Beat until thick enough to spread; add nuts.

SHINING CHOCOLATE FROSTING

Very smooth and shiny.
Frosts one 2-layer, 9-inch cake or 2 dozen cupcakes

2 tablespoons butter
¼ cup light corn syrup
3 tablespoons water
6 ounces (1 cup) semisweet
  chocolate chips

1 teaspoon vanilla extract
2 cups powdered sugar, sifted

Mix first three ingredients over medium heat, stirring constantly. Remove from heat; add chocolate chips. Add vanilla and gradually blend in sugar.

SATINY CHOCOLATE FROSTING

Frosts one 2-layer, 8-inch cake

2 cups powdered sugar, sifted
¼ cup butter, softened
1 tablespoon whipping cream
1 teaspoon vanilla extract

¹⁄₁₆ teaspoon salt
1 egg
2 envelopes premelted unsweetened
  chocolate

Combine first 5 ingredients; beat until well blended. Add egg; beat well. Add premelted chocolate; blend. If too thin add more sugar.

DARK CHOCOLATE FROSTING

Intensely chocolate.
Frosts one 2-layer, 9-inch cake

2 *tablespoons water*
8 *ounces sweet chocolate*

2 *egg yolks*
1 *teaspoon vanilla extract*

Put water and chocolate in saucepan over low heat. Stir until chocolate is melted; remove from heat. Add egg yolks, one at a time, beating well after each addition. Add vanilla and beat again.

∎

CREAMY FUDGE FROSTING

Very rich.
Frosts one 2-layer, 9-inch cake

4½ *ounces (4½ squares) unsweetened*
  chocolate, melted
¼ *cup hot water*
2¼ *cups powdered sugar*

4 *egg yolks*
4 *tablespoons butter*
1 *teaspoon vanilla extract*

Melt chocolate over hot water; remove from heat. Add water and powdered sugar. Add egg yolks separately, beating well after each addition. Add butter, one tablespoon at a time. Add vanilla.

∎

EXTRA-SPECIAL CHOCOLATE FROSTING

Frosts one 2-layer, 8- or 9-inch cake

¼ *cup butter*
¼ *cup whipping cream*
6 *ounces (1 cup) semisweet*
  chocolate chips

1 *egg yolk*
1 *teaspoon vanilla extract*
2 *cups powdered sugar*

Combine butter and cream in saucepan. Bring to boil over moderate heat, stirring constantly; remove from heat. Add chocolate chips; stir until melted and smooth. Stir in egg yolk and vanilla. Gradually beat in sugar; continue to beat until stiff enough to spread.

∎

MILK CHOCOLATE TOPPING

Frosts one 2-layer, 9-inch cake

4 ounces sweet milk chocolate
1 egg

1 cup whipping cream, whipped
1 teaspoon vanilla extract

Melt chocolate over hot water. Add egg, beating until blended; cool slightly. Add whipped cream; fold in vanilla.

·

SEVEN-MINUTE
CHOCOLATE FROSTING

Lightened with egg whites.
Frosts one 2-layer, 8- or 9-inch cake

2 egg whites
3½ ounces (3½ squares) unsweetened chocolate, melted

2¼ cups sugar
½ teaspoon butter
½ teaspoon vanilla extract

Beat egg whites until stiff; stir in 3 ounces melted chocolate, which has been slightly cooled, and 2 cups sugar. Spread between layers, on top and sides of a 8- or 9-inch cake. Melt remaining ½ ounce chocolate with butter; cool. Add vanilla and remaining sugar; mix well. Dipping the tip of a teaspoon in the chocolate, form half moon swirls in frosting.

·

GREAT MARSHMALLOW
FUDGE ICING

Frosts one 2-layer, 9-inch cake

12 marshmallows, finely cut up
3 ounces (3 squares) unsweetened chocolate
2 tablespoons butter

¼ cup cold water
1 teaspoon vanilla extract
2 cups powdered sugar

Heat first four ingredients over low heat until melted, stirring constantly. Remove from heat. Add vanilla and sugar all at once. Beat until correct consistency to spread over cake.

·

CHOCOLATE CAKE ICING

A richer marshmallow frosting.
Frosts one 2-layer, 8-inch cake

4 tablespoons butter
1 ounce (1 square) unsweetened
chocolate
½ cup brown sugar, firmly packed

2 tablespoons light corn syrup
3 tablespoons whipping cream
½ cup powdered sugar, sifted
½ cup miniature marshmallows

Mix butter, chocolate, brown sugar, corn syrup and whipping cream in a saucepan; bring to a boil. Stirring constantly, boil hard about 2 minutes or until bubbles are glossy; remove from heat. Mix in powdered sugar and marshmallows; stir until melted.

CHOCOLATE FONDUE FROSTING

Also makes a quick coating for cookies, doughnuts and crackers.
Frosts one 2-layer, 9-inch cake

1 can prepared fudge frosting

1 cup miniature marshmallows

Combine both in saucepan; stir over low heat until marshmallows melt.

CHOCOLATE BUTTER CREAM

Frosts one 2-layer, 8-inch cake

4½ ounces (¾ cup) semisweet
chocolate chips
¼ cup water
1 teaspoon instant coffee

¼ cup sugar
4 egg yolks
½ cup unsalted butter
½ teaspoon vanilla extract

Place chocolate chips, water, coffee and sugar together in top of double boiler over simmering water; stir in egg yolks one at a time. Cook, stirring until thickened, about 3 minutes. Cool until lukewarm. Cream butter. Add to chocolate mixture, beating until smooth. Add vanilla. If necessary, chill to reach spreading consistency.

MOCHA ICING

Frosts one 2-layer, 9-inch cake

⅓ cup butter
3 heaping cups powdered sugar
¼ teaspoon salt
1½ ounces (1½ squares) unsweetened
   chocolate, melted

½ cup coffee, double strength
½ teaspoon vanilla extract

Cream butter. Sift together sugar and salt. Add ½ of sugar mixture to butter, blending well. Add chocolate; stir well. Add remaining sugar alternately with coffee, beating after each addition until smooth and right consistency to spread. Add vanilla.

BUTTER
PEPPERMINT-CHOCOLATE ICING

Frosts one 2-layer, 9-inch cake

2 ounces (2 squares) semisweet
   chocolate
2 tablespoons butter
¼ cup hot water

1/16 teaspoon salt
½ teaspoon peppermint extract
2 cups powdered sugar, sifted

Melt chocolate with butter over low heat. Blend in water and salt; remove from heat. Cool. Add peppermint extract. Stir in powdered sugar; beat until smooth and thick.

COCOA PEPPERMINT FROSTING

Buttery, with crushed peppermint candy.
Frosts on 2-layer, 9-inch cake

⅓ cup butter
½ cup cocoa
3 cups powdered sugar, sifted
½ cup milk, scalded

¾ teaspoon peppermint extract
1 tablespoon peppermint candy,
   finely crushed

Melt butter in saucepan over medium heat; stir in cocoa. Blend in remaining ingredients. Place pan in bowl of ice water. Beat until proper consistency to spread, 5 to 6 minutes.

CHOCOLATE SOUR CREAM FROSTING

Excellent for spice cakes.
Frosts one single-layer, 10 × 15-inch cake

4½ ounces (¾ cup) semisweet
   chocolate chips
½ cup sour cream, room
   temperature

¹⁄₁₆ teaspoon salt

Melt chocolate over hot water; cool until lukewarm. Blend in sour cream. Add salt.

■

VELVETY CHOCOLATE FROSTING

Imitation sour cream provides tangy flavor without richness.
Frosts one 2-layer, 9-inch cake

6 ounces (1 cup) semisweet
   chocolate chips
1 teaspoon vanilla extract

¼ teaspoon salt
¼ cup imitation sour cream
2 cups powdered sugar, sifted

Melt chocolate chips over hot water; stir until smooth. Remove from heat. Blend in next three ingredients; gradually beat in sugar.

■

CARRIE'S CREAM CHOCOLATE FROSTING

Frosts one single-layer, 9 × 9-inch or one 2-layer 8- or 9-inch cake

4 ounces sweet chocolate
⅓ cup cream cheese
1 tablespoon whipping cream
1 cup powdered sugar, sifted

¼ teaspoon salt
½ teaspoon vanilla extract
¼ teaspoon almond extract

Melt chocolate in top of double boiler over hot water. Cool slightly. Add cream cheese and whipping cream; blend well. Gradually add sugar; mix well. Add salt and vanilla and almond extracts.

■

MOCHA CREAM CHEESE TOPPING

Rich, creamy, and coffee flavored.
Frosts one 2-layer 9-inch cake or 2 dozen cupcakes

2 ounces (2 squares) semisweet
  chocolate, melted
2/3 cup cream cheese
1 tablespoon instant coffee
4 tablespoons brown sugar, packed
  firmly

1/16 teaspoon salt
1 egg, separated
1 teaspoon vanilla extract
1 cup whipping cream, whipped

Blend melted chocolate, cream cheese, coffee, 2 tablespoons brown sugar and salt. Beat in egg yolk and vanilla. Beat egg white until stiff but not dry; gradually add remaining brown sugar. Fold this and whipped cream into the coffee chocolate mixture.

Fillings

⋮

CHOCOLATE DREAM FILLING

Gelatin adds body to this filling.
Fills one 2-layer, 9-inch cake

1/2 teaspoon unflavored gelatin
1 tablespoon cold water
1/4 cup superfine sugar

2 tablespoons cocoa
1/2 cup whipping cream, whipped

Soften gelatin in water in top of double boiler. Place over boiling water; stir until gelatin is dissolved. Combine sugar and cocoa; stir into whipped cream. Add dissolved gelatin; blend well. Whip with electric mixer until thick. Chill thoroughly.

CHOCOLATE WHIPPED CREAM

Fills 3 cakes

1 cup whipping cream
3 ounces (½ cup) semisweet
    chocolate chips

¼ teaspoon salt
½ teaspoon vanilla extract
¼ teaspoon almond extract

Combine whipping cream and chocolate chips; heat over very low heat until chocolate melts. Chill thoroughly; add salt and vanilla and almond extracts. Beat until thick and fluffy. Refrigerate until ready to use.

CREAMY CHOCOLATE FILLING

Filling and/or frosting with an additional glaze.
Fills and frosts one 2-layer, 8-inch cake

6 ounces (1 cup) semisweet
    chocolate chips
½ cup light corn syrup
2 tablespoons water

1 cup whipping cream, whipped
    until stiff
1 teaspoon vanilla extract

Melt chocolate over hot, not boiling water. Stir in corn syrup and water; mix until smooth. Reserve ¼ of this mixture for glaze. Into remaining mixture fold whipping cream, which has been mixed with vanilla. After filling and frosting cake, pour glaze over top.

CHOCOLATE BUTTER FILLING

Fills one 2-layer, 9-inch cake

3 ounces (½ cup) semisweet
    chocolate chips
2 tablespoons water, boiling
2 egg yolks

2 tablespoons powdered sugar
¼ cup butter, softened
1 teaspoon black walnut flavoring

Place chocolate chips in small mixing bowl; add boiling water and blend. Add remaining ingredients and blend at highest speed of mixer until smooth.

Glazes

FUDGY GLAZE

Perfect for eclairs and pound cakes.
Makes about 2½ cups

5 ounces (5 squares) unsweetened
  chocolate
½ cup butter

5 cups powdered sugar
1 13-ounce can evaporated milk
1¼ teaspoons vanilla extract

Melt chocolate and butter over low heat; remove from heat. Add 3 cups sugar, alternating with milk. Blend well after each addition. Bring to boil over medium heat, stirring constantly. Cook until mixture thickens and is creamy, 8 to 10 minutes. Remove from heat; stir in vanilla. Cool to lukewarm; add remaining sugar, blending well.

•

MIXED FRUIT CHOCOLATE GLAZE

Makes 1¾ cups

½ cup mixed candied fruit, chopped
¼ cup water
6 ounces (1 cup) semisweet
  chocolate chips

¼ teaspoon almond extract

Mix fruit and water. Melt chocolate chips over hot water; stir into fruit mixture. Add almond extract. Serve warm or cool.

•

CHOCOLATE MARMALADE GLAZE

Shiny and orange flavored.
Makes 1⅔ cups

6 ounces (1 cup) semisweet
  chocolate chips

⅓ cup hot water
1 cup marmalade

Mix chocolate chips and hot water together over medium heat until chocolate is melted. Stir in marmalade.

CHOCOLATE TOPPING GLAZE

A really attractive, shiny glaze.
Makes about ⅓ cup

2 tablespoons cocoa
1 tablespoon plus 2 teaspoons water
1 tablespoon butter

1 tablespoon corn syrup
1 cup powdered sugar

Heat all ingredients together except sugar; stir until smooth. Remove from heat. Beat in sugar. Drizzle over cake.

·

CHOCOLATE GLAZE À LA RUM

Makes about 1⅔ cups

1½ cups powdered sugar, sifted
2½ ounces sweet chocolate, ground

1 tablespoon rum
1 tablespoon warm water

Combine all ingredients; stir until smooth.

·

MOCHA GLAZE

Makes about 1½ cups

2 tablespoons cocoa
1 tablespoon plus 2 teaspoons
   coffee

1 teaspoon butter
1 tablespoon corn syrup
1 cup powdered sugar, sifted

Combine all ingredients, except sugar. Cook over low heat, stirring until mixture is smooth. Remove from heat; beat in sifted sugar.

·

CHAPTER FIVE

PIES AND
PIE CRUSTS

Pies

JEAN'S CHOCOLATE ANGEL PIE

Makes one 8-inch pie

MERINGUE CRUST
- 2 egg whites, yolks reserved for filling
- ⅛ teaspoon cream of tartar
- ⅛ teaspoon salt
- ½ cup sugar
- ½ teaspoon vanilla extract
- ½ cup walnuts, chopped

FILLING
- ½ cup butter
- ¾ cup sugar
- 1 ounce (1 square) unsweetened chocolate, melted
- 1 teaspoon vanilla
- 2 eggs plus 2 yolks
- Whipped cream

Preheat oven to 275°. Grease an 8-inch pie pan. For meringue, beat egg whites with cream of tartar and salt until very stiff. Gradually add sugar and vanilla. Stir in walnuts. Spread over bottom and sides of pan. Bake until dry but not colored, about 55 minutes. Turn off heat and cool in oven. For filling, cream butter and sugar; add melted chocolate and vanilla. Add eggs one at a time, beating 5 minutes after each addition, then beat in extra yolks. Pour into meringue shell. Chill. Cover with whipped cream.

CHOCOLATE DELIGHT PIE

A lighter chocolate pie.
Makes one 8-inch pie

- 1 cup prepared cocoa
- ¼ cup sugar
- 4 tablespoons cornstarch
- ⅛ teaspoon salt

- 1½ cups milk
- ½ cup whipping cream, whipped
- 1 8-inch pie shell, baked

Mix first four ingredients in saucepan; gradually stir in milk. Stir until smooth. Bring to a boil, stirring constantly, over low heat. Continue to cook until thick. Remove from heat. Cover tightly and cool to room temperature. When cool, stir until smooth; fold in whipped cream. Pour into pie shell. Chill until set.

BROWNIE PIE

Makes one 9-inch pie

1¼ cups sweetened condensed milk
¼ teaspoon salt
6 ounces (1 cup) semisweet
   chocolate chips
2 tablespoons flour
1 teaspoon vanilla extract

2 eggs, separated
½ cup nuts, chopped
2 tablespoons sugar
1 9-inch pie shell, unbaked
1 cup whipping cream, whipped

Preheat oven to 350°. Bring condensed milk and salt to a boil over medium heat. Stir constantly. Stir in chocolate chips, flour and vanilla; blend until smooth. Beat in egg yolks one at a time. Stir in nuts. Beat egg whites until stiff but not dry. Add sugar and beat until stiff, glossy peaks form. Fold chocolate mixture into egg white mixture; pour into pie shell. Bake about 45 minutes. Serve cold or warm. Spread whipped cream on top.

CHOCOLATE PIE

Everyone's favorite.
Makes one 9-inch pie

2 ounces (2 squares) unsweetened
   chocolate
2 cups milk
½ teaspoon salt
⅔ cup flour

⅔ cup plus 3 tablespoons sugar
3 eggs, separated
1 tablespoon butter
1 teaspoon vanilla extract
1 9-inch pie shell, baked

Melt chocolate in milk in top of double boiler over boiling water; beat until blended. Combine salt, flour and all but 3 tablespoons sugar; stir slowly into chocolate mixture. Cook until thick, stirring constantly. Cook another 10 minutes, stirring occasionally. Stir small amounts of hot mixture into egg yolks, then pour back into rest of hot mixture. Beat vigorously. Cook 1 minute. Add butter and vanilla. Cool thoroughly. Pour into pie shell. Beat egg whites until stiff, adding remaining sugar. Spread meringue over top to edges of pie. Place under broiler a few moments until lightly browned. Cool.

UNBAKED
CHOCOLATE ALMOND PIE

A milk chocolate shell and a creamy, almond-flavored filling.
Makes one 9-inch pie

1 9¾-ounce milk chocolate bar
1 teaspoon cooking oil
1 cup nuts, finely chopped
½ cup marshmallows

¼ cup milk
1 teaspoon vanilla extract
¼ teaspoon almond extract
1 cup whipping cream, whipped

Line a 9-inch pie pan with aluminum foil. Melt ½ the chocolate bar in cooking oil; stir until smooth. Stir in nuts, blending well. Spread on bottom and sides of pie pan; chill until firm. Lift out of pan; peel off foil. Replace chocolate shell in pie pan. Melt marshmallows, remaining chocolate bar, milk, and vanilla and almond extracts in double boiler over hot water. Remove from heat; cool. Fold in whipped cream. Pour into chocolate shell. Refrigerate overnight.

CHOCOLATE ALMOND
WHIPPED CREAM DESSERT

Makes one 8-inch pie

2 egg whites
⅛ teaspoon cream of tartar
⅛ teaspoon salt
½ cup sugar, sifted
½ cup nuts, finely chopped
1½ teaspoons vanilla extract

1 teaspoon almond extract
4 ounces sweet chocolate
3 tablespoons water
1 cup whipping cream, whipped
¾ cup almond macaroons, crushed

Preheat oven to 300°. Lightly grease an 8-inch pie pan. Beat egg whites until foamy; add cream of tartar and beat until mixture stands in peaks. Add sugar a tablespoon at a time; beat until whites are very stiff. Fold in nuts and ½ teaspoon each vanilla and almond extracts. Spread in pie pan. Make a shell like a bird's nest, bringing sides up about ½ inch over edges. Bake about 60 minutes. Cool. Put chocolate and water in saucepan. Stir constantly over low heat until melted. Cool until thick. Add remaining vanilla, almond extract and whipped cream. Fold in macaroons. Turn into meringue shell. Chill several hours before serving.

CHOCOLATE BANANA CREAM PIE

Makes one 9-inch pie

2 ounces (2 squares) unsweetened
   chocolate
2 cups milk
½ teaspoon salt
⅔ cup flour
1¼ cups sugar
3 egg yolks, slightly beaten

1 tablespoon butter
½ teaspoon vanilla extract
3 ripe bananas, sliced
1 9-inch pie shell, baked
1 cup whipping cream, whipped
   with 3 tablespoons sugar

Melt chocolate in milk in top of double boiler over boiling water; beat until blended. Combine salt, flour and sugar; stir slowly into chocolate mixture. Cook until thick, stirring constantly. Cook 10 minutes more, stirring occasionally. Stir small amounts of hot mixture into egg yolks, then pour back into rest of hot mixture; beat vigorously. Cook 1 minute. Add butter and vanilla. Cool thoroughly. Cover bottom of pie shell with small amount of cooled filling. Place banana slices in pie shell; cover with remaining filling. Spread with sweetened whipped cream and top with remaining banana slices. Chill.

CHOCOLATE BOSTON CREAM PIE

A delicious combination of chilled pudding and cake.
Makes one 8- or 9-inch pie

1 (5½ ounces) package vanilla
   pudding and pie filling mix
2⅓ cups milk
1 ounce (1 square) unsweetened
   chocolate

1 tablespoon unsalted butter
½ teaspoon almond extract
½ cup whipping cream, whipped
1 8- or 9-inch yellow cake layer,
   baked and cooled

Cover the surface of 8- or 9-inch cake pan with waxed paper and chill. Combine pudding mix and milk. Cook over medium heat in small saucepan until mixture comes to full boil; remove from heat. Combine 1 cup hot pudding with chocolate and butter. Add almond extract, stirring well until chocolate is melted. Beat the vanilla pudding until smooth; blend in whipped cream. Split yellow cake layer in two. Place one layer in pan and cover with pudding mix. Place second layer over first. Beat chocolate pudding mix until smooth; spread over top of cake. Chill several hours.

CHOCOLATE THRILLER

Indeed a thriller!
Makes one 9-inch pie

Easy Chocolate Crumb Shell (see following recipe)
1 *cup cream cheese, softened*
½ *cup sugar*
1 *teaspoon vanilla extract*
2 *egg yolks, beaten*

4 *ounces (¾ cup) semisweet chocolate chips, melted*
2 *egg whites*
1 *cup whipping cream*
¾ *cup pecans, chopped*

Prepare Easy Chocolate Crumb Shell. Combine cheese, ¼ cup sugar and vanilla. Stir in egg yolks, and melted chocolate. Beat egg whites until soft peaks form; add ¼ cup sugar; fold into chocolate mixture. Fold in whipped cream and pecans. Pour into crumb shell and freeze.

EASY CHOCOLATE CRUMB SHELL

Makes one 9-inch pie shell

1¼ *cups chocolate wafers, finely crumbled*

5 *tablespoons butter, melted*

Thoroughly mix crumbled wafers with butter. Press evenly into bottom and sides of a 9-inch pie pan to form crumb shell. Chill.

CHOCOLATE CHEESE PIE

A supremely rich pie. Serve in very thin wedges.
Makes one 9- or 10-inch pie

Chocolate Cookie Pie Shell (see following recipe)
2 *cups cream cheese, softened*
1 *cup hoop cheese, softened*
3 *eggs*
½ *cup sugar*

1 *teaspoon lemon juice*
2 *teaspoons vanilla extract*
Sour Cream Topping (see following recipe)
Shaved chocolate (garnish)

Preheat oven to 350°. Prepare Chocolate Cookie Pie Shell. Place softened cheeses in bowl and beat with electric mixer until well blended. Add eggs one at a time, beating well after each addition. Gradually beat in sugar. Add lemon juice and vanilla; blend well. Place into

Chocolate Cookie Pie Shell. Bake 25 to 30 minutes. Cool 10 minutes; spread with Sour Cream Topping. Bake another 10 minutes. Refrigerate overnight. Sprinkle with shaved chocolate pieces.

CHOCOLATE COOKIE PIE SHELL

Makes one 8- or 9-inch pie shell

2 cups chocolate cookie crumbs, finely crushed

⅓ cup butter, softened

Combine cookie crumbs and butter; blend well. Press into bottom and sides of 9- or 10-inch pie pan.

CHOCOLATE SOUR CREAM TOPPING

Makes about 2½ cups

4 tablespoons cocoa
4 tablespoons sugar

2 teaspoons vanilla extract
2 cups sour cream

Add cocoa, sugar and vanilla to sour cream. Mix well; do not whip.

.

CHOCOLATE CRUMB SHELL EGGNOG PIE

Makes one 9-inch pie

1¼ cups chocolate wafers, finely crushed
6 tablespoons butter, melted
1 envelope unflavored gelatin
½ cup cold water

3 eggs
¼ cup sugar
½ cup plus ⅔ cup chilled evaporated milk
1 tablespoon rum flavoring

Grease a 9-inch pie pan. Mix crushed wafers and butter. Press into bottom and sides of pie pan. Soften gelatin in cold water. Beat eggs slightly in top of double boiler. Add sugar and ½ cup evaporated milk. Cook over hot water until thickened, stirring constantly. Dissolve gelatin in hot custard; remove from heat. Add rum flavoring. Cool. When custard is slightly set, whip ⅔ cup chilled evaporated milk until very stiff; fold into custard mixture. Pour custard into pie shell. Refrigerate overnight.

.

CHIFFON CHOCOLATE PIE

Makes one 10-inch pie

2 ounces (2 squares) semisweet
   chocolate
¾ cup water
1 envelope unflavored gelatin
4 eggs, separated
1 cup sugar

¼ teaspoon salt
1 teaspoon vanilla extract
½ teaspoon peppermint extract
   Prepared graham cracker pie
   crust
½ cup whipping cream, whipped

Grease well a 10-inch pie pan. Line with graham cracker pie crust. Melt chocolate in ½ cup water. Add gelatin softened in remaining water. Beat egg yolks; add to chocolate mixture with ½ cup sugar, salt and vanilla and peppermint extracts. Cool. Beat egg whites until stiff; beat in remaining sugar. Fold into chocolate mixture. Spread into graham cracker crust. Refrigerate until cold. Before serving, top with dollops of whipped cream.

CHOCOLATE HONEY PIE

Makes one 8-inch pie

PIE CRUST
1 cup flour
¾ teaspoon salt
¼ cup plus 3 tablespoons butter
3 tablespoons milk
½ cup almonds, slivered

FILLING
6 ounces (1 cup) semisweet
   chocolate chips
2 eggs, separated
½ cup sour cream
⅓ cup honey
1 cup whipping cream, whipped

For pie crust, preheat oven to 450°. Sift together flour and ½ teaspoon salt into mixing bowl; cut in butter until mixture resembles peas. Sprinkle milk over mixture; stir lightly with fork until dough is sufficiently moist to hold together. Form into a ball; flatten to about ½-inch thick. Roll out on floured board to a circle about 2 inches larger than 8-inch pie pan; fit loosely into pan. Fold edges to form a standing rim. Flute edges; prick with fork. Press almonds into bottom of shell. Bake until golden brown, 10 to 12 minutes. Cool. For filling, melt chocolate in top of double boiler over boiling water. Add egg yolks, stirring until mixture leaves sides of pan in a smooth ball; remove from heat. Blend in sour cream and beat until smooth. Set aside. Beat egg whites with remaining salt until stiff, but not dry. Slowly add honey, beating well after each addition. Continue beating until meringue stands in stiff glossy peaks. Fold chocolate-sour cream mixture into egg whites. Place in cooled pie shell. Chill overnight. Place dollops of whipped cream on top; garnish with slivered almonds if desired.

CHOCOLATE FUDGE PEPPERMINT PIE

A great fudge pie shell filled with a creamy peppermint filling.
Makes one 9-inch pie

¼ cup butter, melted
2 cups fudge cake mix
1 egg
1 (14.5 ounces) package fluffy
   white frosting mix, prepared

½ cup boiling water
½ teaspoon peppermint extract
¼ teaspoon vanilla extract
6 drops green food coloring
1 cup whipping cream, whipped

Preheat oven to 350°. Melt butter in large saucepan. Add 2 cups cake mix (dry) and egg. Stir until well mixed; pat into 9-inch pie pan. Bake 10 to 15 minutes (shell will be puffy, but will flatten when cooled). Cool completely. Prepare frosting as directed on package, adding food coloring with boiling water. Fold in whipped cream and vanilla and peppermint extracts. Pour into pie shell. Refrigerate until firm, 5 to 6 hours or overnight.

•

CHOCOLATE RUM PIE

Makes one 10-inch pie

6 egg yolks
1 cup sugar
1 envelope unflavored gelatin
½ cup water
½ cup rum
1 cup whipping cream, beaten until
   stiff

1 10-inch baked pie shell
3 ounces (½ cup) semisweet
   chocolate chips
   Whipped cream
   Chocolate chips (optional)

Beat egg yolks until lemon colored; beat in sugar until thoroughly blended. Place gelatin in water in small saucepan; bring just to boil over low heat, stirring constantly until dissolved. Remove from heat and pour over egg yolk-sugar mixture, stirring constantly. Add rum and stir again. Add whipped cream to this mixture; chill until it starts to set. Add chocolate chips; mix well. Turn into baked pie shell. Chill until completely set. Top with additional whipped cream; sprinkle with additional chocolate chips if desired.

•

CRUNCHY CRUST CHOCOLATE PIE

Makes one 9-inch pie

4½ ounces (¾ cup) semisweet
   chocolate chips
3 tablespoons butter
2 cups Rice Krispies
½ teaspoon vanilla extract

1 quart green mint ice cream,
   slightly softened
1 ounce (1 square) unsweetened
   chocolate, shaved

Grease a 9-inch pie pan. Melt chocolate and butter in top of double boiler. Add cereal and vanilla. Press into bottom and sides of pie pan; chill. Fill with alternating layers of ice cream and shaved chocolate. Freeze. Let stand 10 minutes before serving.

MOCHA CREAM PIE

Makes one 9-inch pie

Cocoa-Nut Shell (see following
   recipe)
6 ounces (1 cup) semisweet
   chocolate chips
¼ cup water
4 teaspoons instant coffee
⅛ teaspoon salt

1 cup marshmallow cream
2 egg whites
1 cup whipping cream
1 teaspoon vanilla extract
¼ teaspoon almond extract
¼ teaspoon black walnut flavoring
1 cup whipping cream, whipped

Prepare Cocoa-Nut Shell. Stir chocolate chips, water, instant coffee and salt over hot water until blended and smooth; remove from water. Stir in marshmallow cream; set aside. Beat egg whites until stiff but not dry. Whip cream with almond and vanilla extracts and black walnut flavoring; fold into egg whites. Fold in chocolate mixture until well blended. Pile into Cocoa-Nut Shell. Refrigerate until firm, about 4 hours. Garnish pie with dollops of whipped cream.

COCOA-NUT SHELL

Makes one 9-inch pie shell

1 cup cocoa
1 tablespoon butter, melted

1½ cup nuts, finely chopped

Line a 9-inch pie pan with aluminum foil. Mix cocoa and butter; stir until smooth. Discard 2 tablespoons. Stir in nuts until well blended. Spread on bottom and sides of pan. Chill until firm, about 1 hour. Lift out of pan; peel off foil. Replace shell in pie pan.

FARMER'S BLACK BOTTOM PIE

Makes one 9-inch pie

1 cup sugar
⅛ teaspoon salt
3 eggs, separated
1¾ cups milk
2 ounces (2 squares) unsweetened chocolate, chopped
1½ teaspoons vanilla extract
¼ cup water

1 envelope unflavored gelatin
½ cup sugar
1 tablespoon rum flavoring
½ cup whipping cream
4 ounces sweet cooking chocolate, shaved
1 9-inch pie shell, baked

Mix sugar, salt and egg yolks in top of double boiler. Stir in milk. Cook over hot water until slightly thick, stirring constantly. Measure out a cup of mixture, reserving the rest. Stir chopped chocolate and vanilia extract into 1 cup of mixture until smooth and chocolate is melted. Pour into pie shell. Place gelatin in water; let stand 5 to 6 minutes. Stir into reserved custard until gelatin is completely melted. Cool. Beat egg whites until foamy. Beat in sugar about 2 tablespoons at a time, beating well after each addition, until egg whites form stiff peaks. Fold in cooled custard, then rum. Chill until mixture stands in soft mounds. Carefully place on chocolate layer in pie shell. Chill until set (several hours at least). Whip cream and cover top of pie; sprinkle with shaved chocolate.

ROSE'S BLACK BOTTOM PIE

Another, quicker version of the black bottom pie.
Makes one 9-inch pie

1 (8½ ounces) box chocolate wafers
1 tablespoon unflavored gelatin
¼ cup cold water
2 eggs, separated
½ cup sugar

1/16 teaspoon salt
2 cups milk
2 teaspoons vanilla extract
1 cup whipping cream, whipped

Line a 9-inch ovenproof glass pie plate with chocolate wafers. Dissolve gelatin in water. Beat egg yolks with sugar and salt. Scald milk; pour over egg mixture. Cook in top of double boiler until thick. Add dissolved gelatin. When cool, add vanilla. Beat egg whites until stiff; gently fold in. Pour mixture over wafers. Refrigerate at least 4 hours. Serve with whipped cream.

MOTHER'S CHOCOLATE PECAN PIE

Makes one 9-inch pie

⅔ cup evaporated milk
2 tablespoons butter
4½ ounces (¾ cup) semisweet
    chocolate chips
2 eggs, slightly beaten
1 cup sugar
2 tablespoons flour

¼ teaspoon salt
1 teaspoon vanilla extract
½ teaspoon black walnut flavoring
1 cup pecans, chopped
8 pecan halves
1 9-inch pie shell, unbaked

Preheat oven to 375°. Mix evaporated milk, butter and chocolate chips in saucepan. Stir over very low heat until chocolate melts; set aside. Mix eggs with sugar, flour and salt. Add chocolate mixture, vanilla and black walnut flavoring and chopped pecans. Mix well. Place mixture in pie shell; arrange pecan halves in circle on top. Bake until firm, 30 to 35 minutes. Cool before serving.

CHOCOLATE CREAM COFFEE PIE

This has a custard-style filling.
Makes one 9-inch pie

1 envelope unflavored gelatin
2 tablespoons cold water
½ cup milk
2 tablespoons sugar
1/16 teaspoon salt
1 teaspoon vanilla extract

1 egg yolk
2⅔ ounces sweet chocolate
¼ cup coffee, double strength
2 cups whipping cream, whipped
1 9-inch pie shell, baked

Soften gelatin in water. Bring milk to boil in top of double boiler. Beat sugar, salt, ½ teaspoon vanilla and egg yolk together until light and creamy. Add a small amount of boiled milk to egg mixture; blend well. Return to remaining milk; cook and stir over hot water until mixture just reaches a boil. Remove from heat. Stir in gelatin until dissolved. Grate nearly all of the chocolate. Add to custard, stirring over hot water until chocolate is melted. Add coffee. Remove from heat; beat with rotary beater until custard is smooth. Chill until custard is consistency of cream. Fold 1 cup of whipped cream into the custard with remaining vanilla. Place in baked pie shell; chill until firm, about 4 hours. Before serving, spread remaining whipped cream over filling. Shave remaining chocolate over top as garnish.

FLUFFY CHOCOLATE RICE PIE

If you like rice pudding, you'll love this.
Makes one 9-inch pie

1 envelope unflavored gelatin
¼ teaspoon salt
¼ cup sugar
2 cups rice, cooked
1 cup cold water
1 egg, lightly beaten

6 ounces (1 cup) semisweet chocolate chips
¼ cup mixed candied fruit, finely chopped
1 cup whipping cream, whipped
1 9-inch pie shell, baked

Combine first three ingredients in a saucepan; mix well. Add rice, ½ cup water and egg; bring just to a boil over medium heat, stirring constantly. Remove from heat; stir in chocolate chips. Gradually add remaining water and mixed fruit. Fold in whipped cream. Chill, stirring occasionally, until mixture starts to hold its shape. Spoon into pie shell. Chill several hours or overnight.

NANCY'S RICH CHOCOLATE PIE

An easy-to-make filling in a chocolate graham cracker crust.
Makes one 9-inch pie

Chocolate Pie Crust (see following recipe)
½ cup unsalted butter
1 cup powdered sugar

2 ounces (2 squares) unsweetened chocolate, melted
2 eggs
½ teaspoon peppermint extract

Prepare Chocolate Pie Crust. Cream butter; add sugar, chocolate and eggs. Pour into crust. Chill 6 hours.

CHOCOLATE PIE CRUST

Makes one 9-inch pie crust

18 graham crackers, crushed
¼ cup brown sugar, firmly packed
2 ounces sweet chocolate, finely chopped

⅓ cup butter, melted
2 teaspoons vanilla extract

Preheat oven to 325°. Grease bottom of 9-inch pie pan with butter. Mix crushed graham crackers with sugar and chocolate, reserving 2 tablespoons chocolate for garnish. Melt butter with vanilla. Add to chocolate mixture, mixing well. Line bottom and sides of pie pan. Bake 10 to 12 minutes. Cool.

SOUTHERN CHOCOLATE PIE

Makes one 9- or 10-inch pie

4 ounces sweet chocolate
¼ cup butter
1 (15 ounces) can evaporated milk
1½ cups sugar
3 tablespoons cornstarch
⅛ teaspoon salt
2 eggs
1 teaspoon vanilla or almond extract

1⅓ cups coconut, flaked
½ cup nuts, finely chopped
1 9-inch pie shell, unbaked*
Whipped cream (optional)
Chopped nuts (optional)

Preheat oven to 375°. Melt chocolate with butter in saucepan over low heat; stir until blended. Remove from heat. Slowly stir in evaporated milk; set aside. Mix sugar, cornstarch and salt. Add eggs and vanilla or almond extract; mix well. Gradually blend chocolate mixture into egg mixture. Pour into pie shell. Mix coconut and nuts; sprinkle over filling. Bake until top is puffy and starts to crack, about 45 minutes. Center of pie will be soft. Cool overnight or at least 5 hours before serving. Garnish with whipped cream and additional nuts if desired.

Flute pie shell with a high rim as there is ample filling for this pie or use a 10-inch pie pan.

SPICY CHOCOLATE PIE

Makes one 9-inch pie

1¼ cups sugar
⅓ cup cocoa
1½ tablespoons arrowroot
½ teaspoon allspice
½ teaspoon salt
¼ cup cold milk

2 cups whipping cream, scalded
3 tablespoons butter
3 eggs, separated
1 teaspoon vanilla extract
1 9-inch pie shell, baked and chilled

Preheat oven to 300°. Mix ½ cup sugar with cocoa, arrowroot, allspice and ¼ teaspoon salt in top of double boiler. Add cold milk; blend until it becomes a smooth paste. Stir in scalded whipped cream and cook over hot water, stirring constantly until mixture is thick and smooth, 4 to 5 minutes. Cover. Cook 7 to 8 minutes more, stirring occasionally, until mixture is very thick. Stir in butter. Beat egg yolks and ½ cup sugar together. Add a little of hot mixture to eggs. Stir eggs into remaining hot mixture. Cook, uncovered, over hot water until very thick, stirring constantly. Stir in vanilla and cool. Pour into pie shell. Beat egg whites until very stiff; add remaining salt. Beat in sugar a tablespoon at a time, beating after each addition until whites stand in stiff peaks. Spread over top of pie. Place in oven until lightly browned, 15 to 20 minutes.

■

CHOCOLATE MERINGUE PIE

Wonderful to behold; serve for a special occasion.
Makes one 8- or 9-inch pie

Meringue Layers (see following recipe)
4½ ounces (¾ cup) semisweet chocolate chips

16 ounces (2 cups) marshmallows
1 (5⅓ ounces) can evaporated milk
1 cup nuts, finely chopped
1 cup whipping cream, whipped

Prepare Meringue Layers. Slowly melt chocolate chips and marshmallows in milk; cool. Add whipped cream and nuts. Place in refrigerator. When ready to serve, spread ⅓ on each of 3 Meringue Layers. Place one on top of the other to form 3-layer pie.

MERINGUE LAYERS

Makes three 8- or 9-inch meringue layers

9 egg whites
¾ teaspoon salt

1¾ cups sugar

Preheat oven to 325°. Lightly butter three 8- or 9-inch pie pans. Beat eggs whites until stiff, but not dry; add salt. Add sugar 1 tablespoon at a time, beating well after each addition. Spread evenly over bottom and sides of pans. Bake for 20 minutes or until dry but not colored. Remove from oven. Let cool, but do not refrigerate.

■

PAULA'S GRASSHOPPER PIE

Makes one 8-inch pie

1½ cups chocolate wafers, crumbled
⅓ cup butter, softened
3 tablespoons sugar
24 marshmallows
½ cup milk

¼ cup green crème de menthe
½ cup white crème de cacao
1 cup whipping cream, whipped
Shaved chocolate curls (optional)

Blend wafer crumbs, butter and sugar. Reserve a few spoonfuls of this mixture for garnish. Press remaining mixture in bottom and sides of 8-inch pie pan. Chill while preparing filling. Mix marshmallows and milk; heat until marshmallows melt. Stir in crème de menthe and crème de cacao. Add whipped cream. Pile into pie shell. Garnish with reserved crumbs and shaved chocolate curls if desired. Refrigerate overnight.

Pie Crusts

CHOCOLATE NUT SHELL

Makes one 8-inch pie shell

1 egg white
1/16 teaspoon salt
1/16 teaspoon cream of tartar

¼ cup sugar
2 tablespoons cocoa
1½ cups nuts, finely chopped

Preheat oven to 500°. Grease well an 8-inch pie pan. Beat egg whites until stiff but not dry. Add salt and cream of tartar. Mix cocoa with sugar; then gradually add mixture to egg whites, beating until stiff glossy peaks form. Add nuts; blend well. Spread over bottom and sides of pie pan. Prick all over with fork. Bake until lightly browned, about 12 minutes. Cool and fill.

MERINGUE SHELL

A fragile, lovely pie shell.
Makes one 8- or 9-inch pie shell

3 egg whites
¼ teaspoon salt

9 tablespoons sugar

Preheat oven to 325°. Lightly grease an 8- or 9-inch pie pan. Beat egg whites until stiff but not dry; add salt. Add sugar 1 tablespoon at a time, beating well after each addition. Spread evenly over bottom and sides of pan. Bake until dry but not colored, about 20 minutes. Remove from oven. Let cool; do not refrigerate.

·

COCONUT CHOCOLATE PIE CRUST

Makes one 9-inch pie crust

2 ounces (2 squares) unsweetened
  chocolate
2 tablespoons butter
½ teaspoon vanilla extract

2 tablespoons hot water
⅔ cup powdered sugar, sifted
1½ cups shredded coconut, toasted

Grease bottom and sides of a 9-inch pie pan. Melt chocolate, butter and vanilla over hot water; stir until well blended. Mix water with sugar; add to chocolate mixture, stirring until well mixed. Add coconut and continue mixing. Spread over bottom and sides of pie pan. Chill until firm.

·

CHOCOLATE PIE SHELL

A solid chocolate shell.
Makes one 8- or 9-inch pie shell

6 ounces (1 cup) semisweet
  chocolate chips

1 tablespoon butter

Preheat oven to 350°. Place chocolate chips and butter in 8- or 9-inch pie pan. Place in oven; heat 2 to 3 minutes. Remove from oven; stir and blend until mixture is smooth. Spread over bottom of pan. Chill 5 to 6 minutes until mixture is slightly thick. Spread sides with back of spoon, being careful to coat pan evenly. Chill and fill.

·

UNBAKED CHOCOLATE CRUST

Makes one 8- or 9-inch pie crust

2 (1 ounce) envelopes premelted
    unsweetened chocolate
¼ cup butter, softened
1 cup graham cracker crumbs

1 cup powdered sugar, sifted
½ teaspoon vanilla extract
1 tablespoon water

Line an 8- or 9-inch pie pan with aluminum foil. Blend chocolate and butter together. Add last four ingredients; blend well. Chill about an hour. Remove crust; peel off foil. Replace crust in pie pan. Fill.

MOCHA SHELL

Makes one 9-inch pie shell

1½ cups graham cracker crumbs
⅓ cup butter, melted
¼ cup brown sugar, firmly packed

2 tablespoons cocoa
⅛ teaspoon allspice
1 tablespoon instant coffee

Mix ingredients together. Press mixture into bottom and sides of a 9-inch pie pan. Chill.

CHAPTER SIX

PUDDINGS

CHOCOLATE CORNSTARCH PUDDING

Basic, satisfying chocolate pudding.
Makes 4 servings

2 ounces (2 squares) unsweetened
 chocolate, melted
2 cups evaporated milk
1⅓ cups water
2 tablespoons cornstarch

½ cup sugar
½ teaspoon salt
2 eggs, beaten
1 teaspoon vanilla extract

Melt chocolate over hot water. Combine evaporated milk and 1 cup water. Add to chocolate and heat. Mix cornstarch, sugar and salt with remaining water. Add to chocolate mixture and cook over hot water, stirring constantly until thick. Cover and cook 20 minutes. Add hot mixture to beaten eggs; add vanilla. Pour into 6-inch mold. Chill.

·

STEAMED CHOCOLATE PUDDING

Makes 10 to 12 servings

3 ounces (3 squares) unsweetened
 chocolate, melted
2 cups flour, sifted
¼ teaspoon salt
½ teaspoon baking soda
2 teaspoons baking powder

⅓ cup butter, softened
1 cup sugar
1 egg
1 cup milk
1 teaspoon vanilla extract
½ teaspoon almond extract

Melt chocolate over hot water. Sift together dry ingredients. Cream butter and sugar together; beat until light and fluffy. Add melted chocolate and egg; mix and beat until smooth. Add flour mixture alternately with the milk, a little at a time, beating well after each addition. Beat in vanilla and almond extracts. Place in 6-cup mold. Cover tightly with plastic wrap. Place mold on rack in pan with about an inch of boiling water. Cover and steam pudding about 2 hours, adding boiling water as it evaporates. Keep pudding in mold about 5 minutes; remove cover. Remove from mold.

·

FRENCH CHOCOLATE-COFFEE PUDDING

Rich and definitely coffee flavored.
Makes 4 to 6 servings

6 ounces (1 cup) semisweet
  chocolate chips
4 egg yolks, beaten
1 cup coffee, double strength

1 teaspoon vanilla extract
2 tablespoons sugar
½ cup whipping cream, whipped

Lightly grease a 6-inch mold or 4 to 6 custard cups. Melt chocolate and coffee in top of double boiler. Remove from heat. Add yolks, stirring until thick. Add sugar and vanilla. Pour into mold or custard cups. Chill in refrigerator. Top with dollops of whipped cream.

•

CHOCOLATE BREAD CUSTARD PUDDING

Nothing is as heartwarming as bread pudding—especially this one.
Makes 4 to 5 servings

2 ounces (2 squares) unsweetened
  chocolate
2¼ cups milk
2 eggs
⅔ cup sugar

¼ teaspoon salt
1 teaspoon vanilla extract
4 slices stale white bread, crusts
  removed
2 tablespoons powdered sugar

Preheat oven to 350°. Grease a 2-quart casserole. Cut bread into cubes; set aside. Mix chocolate and milk in saucepan; stir over medium heat until chocolate is melted. Remove from heat; beat until well blended. Set aside. Beat eggs; stir in sugar and salt. Gradually add chocolate mixture. Stir vigorously; blend in vanilla. Place bread in casserole; pour chocolate-egg mixture over it. Let stand a few minutes. Place casserole in pan of hot water; place pan in oven. Bake until pudding is firm, about 45 minutes. Sprinkle with powdered sugar. Serve warm or cool.

•

CHOCOLATE BREAD PUDDING

Another version with nuts.
Makes 6 servings

1 cup soft bread crumbs
2 cups milk, scalded
1 cup nuts, finely chopped
2 eggs, separated
⅔ cup sugar
½ teaspoon salt

1 lemon, juice and grated peel
2 ounces (2 squares) unsweetened
 chocolate, melted
1 tablespoon whipping cream
½ cup whipping cream, whipped
2 tablespoons powdered sugar

Preheat oven to 350°. Grease a 2-quart casserole. Mix bread crumbs and milk; add nuts, egg yolks, which have been well beaten, sugar, salt and lemon juice and peel. Beat egg whites until stiff but not dry; fold into first mixture. Add melted chocolate blended with cream. Pour into casserole. Bake 30 minutes. Serve with whipped cream sweetened with powdered sugar.

CHOCOLATE CHIP
COTTAGE PUDDING

Makes 8 servings

2 cups flour, sifted
2 teaspoons baking powder
½ teaspoon salt
3 tablespoons butter
1 cup sugar

1 cup milk
½ teaspoon vanilla extract
4½ ounces (¾ cup) semisweet
 chocolate chips
1 cup whipping cream, whipped

Preheat oven to 350°. Grease, line with waxed paper and grease again an 8 × 8 × 2-inch pan. Sift together flour, baking powder and salt 3 times. Cream butter; gradually add sugar. Cream together well. Add flour alternately with milk, a little at a time. Beat after each addition until smooth. Add vanilla. Pour about ⅓ of batter into pan. Sprinkle ⅓ of chocolate chips over batter; repeat, ending with chocolate chips. Bake about 45 minutes. Serve hot, topped with whipped cream.

CHOCOLATE
DEVIL'S FOOD PUDDING

Makes 6 to 8 servings

1 (18.25 ounces) package devil's   *½ cup whipping cream, whipped*
   food cake mix

Grease a 4-cup pudding mold. Mix devil's food mix according to package directions. Fill mold about ¾ full; cover tightly. Place mold on a rack in a larger pan filled with enough boiling water to come halfway up the sides of the mold. Lower heat until water is gently boiling and steam 90 minutes. Unmold. Serve hot with whipped cream.

NEW JERSEY
CHOCOLATE RICE PUDDING

Makes 3 to 4 servings

2 cups rice, cooked   *½ teaspoon salt*
½ cup sugar   *1 teaspoon vanilla extract*
2 cups milk   *½ teaspoon almond extract*
4 tablespoons cocoa   *½ cup whipping cream, whipped*

Wash rice well. Heat milk in top of double boiler over boiling water; add rice. Add cocoa mixed with sugar and salt. Cook until thick. Add vanilla and almond extracts. Serve hot or cold with a dollop of whipped cream on each serving.

CHOCOLATE
PEPPERMINT CHIFFON PUDDING

Makes 4 servings

1 (4½ ounces) package chocolate   *¹⁄₁₆ teaspoon peppermint extract*
   pudding mix   *2 egg whites, beaten until stiff*
2 cups milk

Prepare pudding according to directions on package, but use 2 cups cold milk; cool. Add peppermint extract; fold in egg whites. Pour into 2-cup mold and chill.

CHOCOLATE DATE PUDDING

Makes 6 to 8 servings

1 tablespoon butter
¾ cup sugar
1 egg
1½ cups flour
1½ teaspoons baking powder
½ teaspoon salt
½ cup milk

1 teaspoon vanilla extract
1 ounce (1 square) unsweetened chocolate, melted
½ cup dates, pitted and chopped
½ cup whole dates, pitted
Chocolate Hard Sauce (optional) (see recipe, page 202)

Grease a 10-inch mold. Cream butter and sugar. Add egg, beating well. Sift together dry ingredients; add alternately with milk to creamed mixture. Add vanilla. Melt chocolate over hot water; add, with chopped dates, to ½ of batter. Fill mold about ½ full with alternating spoonfuls of batters. Cover tightly; steam 90 minutes.* Unmold. If desired, stuff whole dates with hard sauce to top pudding. Serve with remaining sauce.

*See instructions for Chocolate Devil's Food Pudding.

▪

MOCHA CRÈME BRULÉE

Delightful and creamy, with a thin, hard shell.
Makes 4 servings

2 egg yolks
1 tablespoon arrowroot
2 tablespoons cocoa
3 tablespoons sugar
2 cups whipping cream

½ cup coffee, double strength
1 teaspoon vanilla extract
½ cup light brown sugar, firmly packed

Combine egg yolks, arrowroot, cocoa and sugar. Gradually stir in cream, then coffee. Cook over very low heat, stirring constantly until pudding thickens; stir in vanilla. Place in ovenproof custard dishes; chill until very cold. Put brown sugar through ricer; spread a layer of brown sugar about ¼-inch thick over surface of pudding. Put under broiler until sugar melts and bubbles.

ROCKY ROAD PUDDING

A perfect, quick dessert that looks as spectacular as it tastes.
Makes 5 to 6 servings

1 (4½ ounces) package chocolate
    pudding and pie filling
1½ cups milk
¼ cup sherry

1 cup marshmallow pieces or
    miniature marshmallows
½ cup walnuts, finely chopped
½ cup whipping cream, whipped

Combine pudding and pie mix with milk and sherry. Cook according to directions on package; cool, stirring now and then. Stir in marshmallows, nuts and whipped cream. Place in sherbet glasses. Chill. Before serving, top each with dollop of whipped cream.

•

CHOCOLATE PEARS SUPREME

A heavenly dessert.
Makes 5 to 6 servings

2¼ cups (12-ounce can) pear halves,
    drained
2 ounces (2 squares) semisweet
    chocolate
¼ cup cocoa
1 cup sour cream

1 cup sugar
1 teaspoon vanilla extract
½ teaspoon almond extract
2 tablespoons crème de cacao

Drain pears; cover and chill. Break chocolate squares into small pieces. Drop a few pieces at a time into blender or mixer (if using blender, drop through top of blender, replacing cover each time). Blend at highest speed a few seconds; turn off mixer or blender. Scrape sides and bottom to be sure all chocolate is off blades. Place in medium bowl. Repeat process until all chocolate is grated. Add cocoa, sour cream and sugar; blend well. Cook in double boiler until thick and smooth, 15 to 20 minutes. Add remaining ingredients. Serve hot over chilled pears.

CHOCOLATE CRACKER PUDDING

Makes 6 to 8 servings

1 cup saltine crackers, slightly broken
3 ounces (3 squares) unsweetened chocolate, grated

1 cup sugar
1 teaspoon vanilla extract
5 eggs
½ cup whipping cream, whipped

Preheat oven to 350°. Butter a shallow 8-inch baking dish (round or square). Beat eggs just enough to break up, not until foamy. Add all other ingredients, blending very little. Pour into baking dish. Bake until knife inserted in center comes out slightly coated, about 25 minutes. Serve hot or cool with whipped cream.

CHOCOLATE SPONGE PUDDING

Delicate, individual sponges with pudding at the bottom.
Makes 8 to 10 servings

2 tablespoons butter
1 cup sugar
1 teaspoon vanilla extract
½ teaspoon almond extract
4 eggs, separated

2 ounces (2 squares) unsweetened chocolate, melted
1 tablespoon arrowroot
1⅓ cups milk
¼ teaspoon salt

Preheat oven to 425°. Grease 8 to 10 custard cups. Cream butter; gradually add sugar, creaming after each addition until fluffy. Add vanilla and almond extracts and egg yolks, one at a time, beating well after each addition. Add chocolate, mixing well. Blend in arrowroot. Add milk; stir until smooth. Beat egg whites; add salt and continue to beat until egg whites stand in soft peaks. Fold in chocolate mixture. Place in custard cups in pan with hot water. Bake until completely puffed across top, 15 to 20 minutes. Refrigerate pudding overnight.

CHAPTER SEVEN

MOUSSES, CREAMS AND SOUFFLÉS

Mousses

BITTER CHOCOLATE MOUSSE

A true chocolate lover's dessert.
Makes 4 to 6 servings

3 eggs, separated
3 tablespoons brandy
1 teaspoon vanilla
½ teaspoon black walnut flavoring
¾ cup plus 1 tablespoon superfine
   sugar

5 ounces (5 squares) unsweetened
   chocolate
4 tablespoons butter
3 tablespoons coffee, double
   strength
½ cup whipping cream, whipped

In top of double boiler, beat egg yolks with brandy, vanilla, black walnut flavoring and ¾ cup sugar until thick and pale yellow. Using electric mixer, continue beating about 5 minutes, over barely simmering water. Remove from heat; allow to reach room temperature. Melt chocolate; remove from heat and stir in butter, then egg mixture. Stir in coffee; whip until foamy. Add remaining tablespoon sugar; beat until stiff. Fold in whipped cream. Pour into 6-inch mold; chill until set.

MOCHA MOUSSE

Makes 4 to 6 servings

4 egg yolks
2 cups whipping cream
1 envelope unflavored gelatin
½ cup sugar
¼ teaspoon salt

2 ounces (2 squares) unsweetened
   chocolate
1 tablespoon instant coffee
¼ cup brandy
1 cup whipping cream, whipped

Beat egg yolks with whipping cream until well mixed. Stir gelatin, sugar and salt in top of double boiler. Add cream mixture; stir in chocolate and coffee. Cook over boiling water until chocolate is melted and coffee dissolved; remove from heat. Add brandy. Beat, using a rotary beater, until chocolate is well blended. Allow to cool. When beginning to thicken, fold in whipped cream. Pour into 4 to 6 serving dishes. Chill until firm.

CHOCOLATE NUT MOUSSE

Makes 6 servings

4½ ounces (¾ cup) semisweet
    chocolate chips
½ cup milk
2 teaspoons unflavored gelatin
2 tablespoons cold water
2 eggs, separated
⅛ teaspoon salt
⅛ teaspoon cream of tartar
3 tablespoons sugar

¼ cup cognac
1½ cups whipping cream, whipped
½ cup toasted nuts, chopped
1 ounce (1 square) semisweet
    chocolate, melted and cooled
½ teaspoon instant coffee
½ teaspoon vanilla extract
12 nut halves (garnish)

Combine chocolate chips and milk over very low heat in heavy saucepan; stir until chocolate melts. Soften gelatin in water. Beat egg yolks slightly; stir in a little of the hot chocolate mixture, return to pan of chocolate mixture and cook, stirring constantly, until mixture thickens slightly; do not boil. Stir gelatin in chocolate mixture until dissolved; cool to room temperature. Beat egg whites with salt and cream of tartar until very stiff; gradually beat in sugar. Stir cognac into cooled chocolate mixture; fold in beaten egg whites, about ¾ of the whipped cream and the chopped nuts. Place in serving bowl. Refrigerate overnight. Fold chocolate and coffee into remaining whipped cream. Place 12 dollops on top of mousse. Garnish with halves of nuts.

FRENCH CHOCOLATE MOUSSE

A sophisticated mousse with crème de cacao.
Makes 10 to 12 servings

½ cup boiling water
8 ounces sweet chocolate
6 tablespoons powdered sugar
6 egg yolks

12 macaroons
18 teaspoons crème de cacao
1 cup whipping cream, whipped

Have ready 10 to 12 parfait glasses. Break chocolate into small pieces in pan; cover with boiling water. Cover pan 5 minutes; pour off water carefully. Stir chocolate with fork while adding powdered sugar. Beat egg yolks; fold in. Refrigerate overnight. Place a macaroon, which has been crushed, in glass. Cover with 1½ teaspoons crème de cacao. Fill each glass with mousse; top with dollop of whipped cream.

CHOCOLATE-COFFEE CREAM MOUSSE

Very creamy and light.
Makes 10 servings

2 envelopes unflavored gelatin
2 cups cold coffee, double strength
3 eggs, separated
¾ cup sugar
1 ounce (1 square) semisweet chocolate

3 tablespoons rum or brandy flavoring
2 cups whipping cream, whipped
Chocolate chips (optional)

Sprinkle gelatin over 1 cup coffee in small bowl; let soften 5 minutes. Using a rotary beater, beat egg yolks with ½ cup sugar in the top of a double boiler until light. Beat in remaining coffee, softened gelatin and chocolate. Cook over simmering water. Stir until mixture coats a metal spoon (chocolate will have melted). Remove from heat; stir in rum or brandy flavoring. Place top of double boiler in pan of ice to cool. Stir often. When mixture is as thick as an unbeaten egg white, stir into whipped cream. Whip egg whites until soft peaks form. Add remaining sugar; beat until stiff. Fold gelatin mixture gently into egg whites until well blended. Place in well-rinsed ring mold. Refrigerate overnight or at least 8 hours. When unmolding run sharp knife around edge of mold; invert over plate. Place a damp, hot cloth over bottom of mold. Shake gently to release; lift off mold. Garnish with remaining whipped cream; sprinkle a few chocolate chips on top if desired.

ROYAL CHOCOLATE MOUSSE

Makes 8 servings

3 ounces (3 squares) unsweetened chocolate
⅓ cup water
¾ cup sugar
⅛ teaspoon salt

3 egg yolks
1 teaspoon vanilla or almond extract
2 cups whipping cream

Combine chocolate and water in a saucepan; bring to a boil over low heat. Stir until blended. Add sugar and salt; simmer 3 to 4 minutes, stirring constantly. Pour this slowly over egg yolks which have been well beaten. Stir well. Cool; then add vanilla or almond extract. Whip cream until soft peaks form; fold into chocolate mixture. Spoon into 4-cup mold. Chill until firm, at least 8 hours.

WINE AND CHOCOLATE MOUSSE

Sweet wine transforms this mousse.
Makes 6 to 8 servings

12 ounces (2 cups) milk chocolate
    chips
½ cup Muscatel wine

4 eggs
2 cups whipping cream

Melt chocolate chips and wine in top of double boiler, stirring constantly until smooth. Beat eggs; add to mixture, blending quickly. Continue to cook for 2 to 3 minutes, stirring; remove from heat. Cool. When cool, whip cream until stiff; fold in wine-chocolate mixture. Place in 2 ice cube trays; freeze until firm. Before serving, cut into squares.

FROZEN CHOCOLATE MOUSSE

Simple, fast, with a hint of orange.
Makes 6 to 8 servings

2 (3¾ ounces) milk chocolate
    almond bars
¼ cup water

¼ teaspoon orange extract
2 cups whipping cream

Soften chocolate bars with water in top of double boiler over hot water, stirring occasionally. Cool slightly; add orange extract. Whip cream until stiff; fold in chocolate mixture. Place in custard cups or large paper cups; cover. Place in freezer overnight.

Creams

BAVARIAN SURPRISE

Very light, but satisfying.
Makes 6 servings

1 envelope unflavored gelatin
⅓ cup cold water

1¼ cups chocolate syrup

Soften gelatin in cold water in saucepan. Stir in ½ the chocolate syrup and cook over medium heat, stirring constantly until gelatin is dissolved. Chill in small bowl until thick, but not set. At low speed of mixer beat until well mixed, scraping sides of bowl often. Gradually beat in remaining chocolate syrup, increasing to high speed. Chill in 3-cup mold. To unmold, dip in hot water for 15 seconds; invert onto plate.

· ·

MOCHA DOT BAVARIAN

The dots are chocolate chips.
Makes 8 servings

1 envelope unflavored gelatin	½ teaspoon vanilla extract
½ cup sugar	½ teaspoon peppermint extract
2 tablespoons instant coffee	1 cup whipping cream, whipped
¹⁄₁₆ teaspoon salt	6 ounces (½ cup) semisweet
2 eggs, separated	chocolate chips, chopped
1¼ cups milk	½ cup nuts, chopped

Lightly grease eight 5-ounce custard cups. Mix together gelatin, ¼ cup sugar, coffee and salt. Add egg yolks and milk. Cook over low heat, stirring until slightly thickened; add vanilla and peppermint extracts. Chill until partially set. Beat egg whites until peaks form, adding remaining sugar. Continue beating until stiff; fold into gelatin mixture. Reserve ½ cup whipped cream and 2 tablespoons chocolate chips for garnish. Fold in remaining whipped cream, chocolate and nuts. Pour into custard cups. Chill until firm. Garnish with reserved whipped cream and chocolate chips.

·

CHOCOLATE RICE BAVARIAN

Makes 6 servings

1 tablespoon unflavored gelatin	1 tablespoon vanilla extract
½ cup cold water	½ teaspoon almond extract
1 cup cooked rice, hot	1 cup whipping cream, whipped
¼ cup sugar	Chocolate sauce of choice
¼ teaspoon salt	(optional)
3 tablespoons cocoa	

Place gelatin and water in a bowl. Place bowl in boiling water; stir until gelatin dissolves. Add rice, sugar, salt, cocoa, and vanilla and almond extract; beat. Cool until mixture starts to thicken. Stir in whipped cream. Place in serving glasses. Chill. Serve with chocolate sauce if desired.

CHOCOLATE
MINT BAVARIAN CREAM

Makes 4 servings

1 tablespoon unflavored gelatin
1 cup prepared Mocha Mix
½ cup water

1 (4½ ounces) package chocolate
  mint pudding and pie filling
Topping (see following recipe)

Grease a 2-cup mold. Soften gelatin in ½ cup Mocha Mix and water. Combine contents of pudding package with remaining Mocha Mix mixture in a saucepan. Cook over medium heat, stirring until mixture comes to a full boil. Add softened gelatin; stir until dissolved. Remove from heat. Chill a few minutes, stirring once or twice. Pour into mold. Chill thoroughly. To unmold, dip in hot water for 15 seconds and invert onto platter. Spread with Topping.

TOPPING

1 cup imitation whipped cream
  topping

¼ cup brown sugar, firmly packed
½ teaspoon vanilla extract

Combine all ingredients and blend well; chill 1 hour. Place in chilled bowl; beat until mixture holds its shape.

CHOCOLATE CHARLOTTE RUSSE

Light, delicate and delicious.
Makes 8 to 10 servings

12 ladyfingers
 2 envelopes unflavored gelatin
 3 cups sugar
½ cup cocoa
¼ teaspoon salt
 3 cups milk

¼ cup brandy
 2 cups whipping cream, whipped
   Whipped cream (garnish)
   Shaved chocolate (garnish)

Split ladyfingers; cut off one end so they will stand upright and place around sides of 8-inch springform pan. Mix gelatin, sugar, cocoa and salt in saucepan; stir in milk. Cook over medium heat, stirring constantly until gelatin and sugar are dissolved, about 5 minutes. Remove from heat; stir in brandy. Chill until mixture mounds slightly when dropped from a spoon. Fold in whipped cream. Place in prepared pan; chill until firm. To unmold, release spring and carefully remove sides of pan. Garnish with additional whipped cream and shaved chocolate.

LIGHT CHOCOLATE
BAVARIAN CREAM

If you're dieting but can't give up chocolate, try this.
Makes 4 to 6 servings

1 (4½ ounces) package chocolate
  pudding and pie filling mix
1 envelope unflavored gelatin
¼ cup sugar
4 teaspoons instant coffee
1½ cups prepared instant nonfat dry
  milk

1 ounce (1 square) unsweetened
  chocolate
2½ cups whipped prepared instant
  nonfat dry milk*

Grease a 1½-quart soufflé mold lightly with oil. Mix pudding mix, gelatin, sugar, coffee and prepared instant nonfat dry milk with chocolate in a saucepan; cook over low heat, stirring constantly. When thickened, cool. Whip cooled pudding; fold into whipped instant nonfat dry milk, blending carefully. Place in mold. Refrigerate overnight.

*To make whipped instant nonfat dry milk, combine ½ cup ice water with ½ cup prepared instant nonfat dry milk in a bowl. Whip about 5 minutes. Add 2 tablespoons lemon juice; continue to beat until firm.

JELLIED MOCHA CRÈME

Makes 4 servings

½ cup sugar
1½ teaspoons freeze-dried coffee
1½ teaspoons cocoa
1 envelope unflavored gelatin
¹⁄₁₆ teaspoon salt

2 cups water, boiling
3 tablespoons coffee liqueur
½ cup whipping cream, whipped
1½ ounces (¼ cup) semisweet
  chocolate chips (garnish)

Have ready 4 dessert glasses. Combine sugar, coffee, cocoa, gelatin and salt in a bowl. Add water, stirring until ingredients are dissolved; cool slightly. Add liqueur. Reserve about ⅔ cup coffee mixture. Divide rest of mixture among 4 dessert glasses. Chill until just set but not firm. Chill remaining coffee mixture until slightly thick; fold into whipped cream. Put a dollop of topping in each glass. Chill until firm. Garnish each serving with a few chocolate chips.

CHOCOLATE CHIP MARSHMALLOW TORTE

Makes 12 servings

½ cup milk
70 miniature marshmallows
2 cups whipping cream
2 ounces (2 squares) unsweetened
    chocolate, grated

2 cups (about 3 dozen) crushed
    graham crackers
¾ cup butter, melted

Grease and line a springform pan with crumbs, reserving some for top of torte. Melt milk and marshmallows in double boiler; cool. Whip cream; fold into grated chocolate. When marshmallow mixture is cool, stir well and fold into whipped cream mixture. Pour into crumb crust; sprinkle top with remaining crumbs. Refrigerate overnight.

DREAMY CHOCOLATE PUDDING

An exquisite, four-layered, rum-flavored delight.
Makes 8 servings

24 ladyfingers
1 cup rum
4 tablespoons whipping cream
8 ounces (8 squares) semisweet
    chocolate
½ teaspoon vanilla extract
1 cup unsalted butter

⅓ cup sugar
2 egg yolks
1 tablespoon orange peel, grated
½ cup candied orange peel
½ cup glacéd cherries
1 cup whipping cream, whipped
    (optional)

Split ladyfingers; arrange in a square on large plate. Sprinkle with rum. Do this at least an hour before preparing pudding (halves should be well soaked in rum, but should keep their shape). Place whipping cream, chocolate and vanilla in top of double boiler; cook over hot water, stirring constantly, until chocolate is melted and mixture is smooth. Cream butter and sugar until fluffy and light and sugar is no longer grainy. Beat in egg yolks, one at a time; add ½ of grated orange peel. Add chocolate mixture a little at a time; beating well after each addition; do not undermix (cream must be completely smooth). Put aside about ⅓ of the chocolate cream. Spread ⅓ of remaining chocolate cream over soaked ladyfingers. Top with another dozen ladyfinger halves and additional cream; top with another layer of each (there will be 4 layers of ladyfingers). Place reserved ⅓ of chocolate over top and sides; smooth surface with wet knife. Decorate with remaining candied orange peel and cherries. Refrigerate overnight. Remove about 45 minutes before serving—this is very important. Place dollop of whipped cream on each serving plate if desired.

CHOCOLATE CHARLOTTE

Makes 6 servings

12 ladyfingers
½ cup Cointreau
1 (4½ ounces) package chocolate
  pudding mix

½ cup whipping cream, whipped

Line bottom and sides of an 8-inch springform pan with split ladyfingers, cutting to fit if necessary. Sprinkle evenly with Cointreau. Make pudding according to directions on package, but eliminate ½ cup milk (to make a thicker pudding). Cool slightly. Spoon into lined pan; chill. When set, unmold on serving dish; spread with whipped cream.

CHOCOLATE CRUMB TORTE

Makes 8 servings

1 cup rice, uncooked
½ cup sugar
½ teaspoon salt
1 teaspoon vanilla extract
½ teaspoon almond extract
3½ cups milk

2 tablespoons butter
3 egg yolks
1 cup whipping cream
½ cup chocolate cookie crumbs

Fresh fruit (optional)

Grease a 9-inch cake pan; sprinkle crumbs over bottom of pan. Combine first 7 ingredients in large saucepan; bring to boil. Stir, then cover and simmer, stirring occasionally, until rice is tender, about 45 minutes. Cool. Beat egg yolks with ¼ cup whipping cream; stir into rice mixture. Spread rice mixture into pan; place in refrigerator several hours. Remove pan. Place torte on dessert dish; cover with remaining cream, which has been whipped until stiff. Arrange fruit on top, if desired.

MOCHA MALLOW FLUFF

Makes 8 servings

1 tablespoon cocoa
1 tablespoon instant coffee
1 cup hot water

48 marshmallows
1 cup whipping cream, whipped
1 cup nuts, chopped

Have ready 8 individual dessert glasses. Stir cocoa, coffee and hot water in a saucepan until blended. Add 36 marshmallows; stir over direct low heat until all marshmallows are thoroughly dissolved. Chill about 1½ hours or until the consistency is thick and syrupy. When thoroughly chilled, beat the mixture at high speed of mixer until doubled in volume. Add whipped cream, remaining marshmallows, which have been cut into quarters, and nuts, folding in gently. Place in dessert glasses. Refrigerate overnight.

PEARS MARTI

Makes 6 servings

6 *whole pears, peeled*
1 *cup sugar*
½ *cup water*
1 *stick cinnamon*
2 *whole cloves*
1 *(4½ ounces) package chocolate pudding mix*

Whipping cream
½ *cup chocolate syrup*
½ *cup nuts, chopped (garnish)*

Leave stems in pears intact. Place pears in a sugar syrup made from boiling sugar and water. Add cinnamon and cloves. Cover and simmer until pears can be pierced with fork but still maintain their shape, 10 to 15 minutes. Drain and cool. Prepare pudding mix, using whipping cream for half the milk. Pour pudding in dessert dishes. Place a pear in center of each. Spoon chocolate syrup over each; sprinkle with chopped nuts.

SPICY MOCHA BOUNCE

Makes 2 servings

¾ *cup coffee, double strength*
¼ *cup sugar*
⅓ *cup chocolate syrup*
1 *cup milk*
2 *scoops chocolate ice cream*

2 *scoops vanilla ice cream*
½ *cup whipping cream, beaten until stiff*
½ *teaspoon allspice, nutmeg or cinnamon*

Combine all ingredients; blend well. Top with whipped cream and dash of spice.

WONDERFUL POTS
OF CHOCOLATE CREAM

These creamy, extra-rich little custards are a classic French dessert.
Makes 4 servings

4 ounces (4 squares) semisweet
    chocolate, melted
4 eggs, separated
⅔ cup raisins

½ teaspoon almond extract
½ cup whipping cream
3 tablespoons powdered sugar

Chill 4 dessert dishes. Melt chocolate. Beat egg yolks one at a time into melted chocolate; stir in raisins and almond extract. Beat egg whites until stiff; carefully fold in raisin-chocolate mixture. Place in 4 dessert dishes. Whip cream with powdered sugar; spread over each serving. Chill.

POT DE CRÈME

An even richer version, without raisins.
Makes 8 servings

8 ounces German sweet chocolate
1½ cups whipping cream
¼ cup sugar

6 egg yolks, slightly beaten
1 teaspoon vanilla extract
½ teaspoon almond extract

Have ready 8 small cups. Melt chocolate in cream in double boiler over hot water; blend in sugar. Gradually stir into egg yolks. Cook over hot water, stirring constantly until mixture resembles thin pudding. Stir in vanilla and almond extracts; pour mixture into 8 cups. Chill.

ARCTIC DESSERT

Makes 12 servings

1 envelope unflavored gelatin
¼ cup cold water
⅔ cup sugar
½ teaspoon salt
1¾ cups milk
4 ounces sweet cooking chocolate

3 eggs, separated
1 teaspoon vanilla extract
1 8-inch single-layer baked devil's
    food cake, cooled
1 cup whipping cream

Soften gelatin in cold water for about 5 minutes. Combine ½ cup sugar, salt and milk in medium saucepan; add chocolate. Cook over medium heat, stirring until chocolate is melted. Beat with rotary beater. Stir a little of the hot mixture into slightly beaten egg yolks; mix well. Return to remaining hot mixture, stirring constantly. Cook over low heat until slightly thickened, 5 to 6 minutes. Remove from heat; add gelatin, stirring until dissolved. Place in large bowl; chill until thick but not set. Stir in vanilla. Beat egg whites until foamy; add remaining sugar, a tablespoon at a time. Continue to beat until stiff, shiny peaks form. Fold into chilled chocolate mixture. Place in large bowl; chill until firm, about 3 hours. Loosen mold at top edge with sharp knife. Place in bowl of warm water a few minutes; remove from water. Shake bowl gently to loosen mold. Place one edge of bowl an inch in from edge of cake layer; unmold onto cake. Prepare whipped cream; spread over top and sides.

Soufflés

∴

RUM CHOCOLATE SOUFFLÉ

Makes 6 servings

2 *envelopes unflavored gelatin*	¾ *cup sugar*
½ *cup water*	2 *tablespoons rum*
2 *squares (2 ounces) unsweetened*	1 *cup whipping cream*
chocolate	*Whipped cream (optional)*
7 *or 8 egg yolks*	

Place gelatin and water in saucepan; let stand about 5 minutes. Add chocolate; cook, stirring, over low heat until chocolate is melted. Remove from heat; set aside. Blend with rotary beater. Beat egg yolks until thick and lemon colored; gradually add sugar. Beat after each addition. Blend in chocolate mixture and rum. Whip cream; fold into mixture. Spoon into 3-cup mold. Chill 3 to 4 hours. If desired, garnish with dollops of whipped cream.

BRUCE'S FAVORITE CHOCOLATE SOUFFLÉ

Makes 12 servings

2 envelopes unflavored gelatin
2 cups milk
1 cup sugar
¼ teaspoon salt
4 eggs, separated

12 ounces (2 cups) semisweet chocolate chips
1 teaspoon vanilla extract
½ teaspoon almond extract
2 cups whipping cream

Grease a 2-quart soufflé dish and make a 2-inch collar* for it. Sprinkle gelatin over milk in saucepan. Add ½ cup sugar, salt, egg yolks and chocolate chips; stir until thoroughly mixed. Place over low heat, stirring constantly until gelatin is dissolved and chocolate melts, 7 to 8 minutes. Remove from heat. Beat with rotary beater until chocolate is blended; stir in vanilla and almond extracts. Chill. Stir occasionally until mixture mounds slightly when dropped from a spoon. Beat egg whites until stiff, but not dry. Add remaining sugar; continue to beat until very stiff. Fold carefully into chocolate mixture. Whip cream; fold into mixture. Place in soufflé dish. Refrigerate overnight.

Fold waxed paper into a 2-inch band, a little longer than circumference of soufflé dish. Tie collar securely around dish and grease inside of collar.

STEAMED CHOCOLATE SOUFFLÉ

Moist, dense and satisfying.
Makes 6 servings

4 ounces sweet chocolate
1 cup milk
3 eggs
4 tablespoons sugar

⅛ teaspoon salt
½ teaspoon vanilla extract
½ teaspoon almond extract
1 cup whipping cream, whipped

Heat chocolate and milk in top of double boiler over boiling water until chocolate is melted; remove from heat. Combine remaining ingredients in a bowl; add a little of the chocolate mixture, stirring constantly. Place back on top of double boiler; add rest of mixture. Cook over boiling water, beating with rotary beater for about 60 seconds. Cover and continue to cook another 20 to 25 minutes. Garnish each serving with a dollop of whipped cream. Serve at once.

SOUFFLÉ AU CHOCOLATE FROID

Airy, light squares adorned with chocolate leaves.
Makes 16 servings

6 ounces (1 cup) semisweet
  chocolate chips
¼ cup water
1 envelope unflavored gelatin
1 cup brown sugar, firmly packed
4 eggs, separated
⅓ cup orange juice

¼ teaspoon salt
1 cup whipping cream, whipped
Chocolate Leaves (see following
  recipe)
Whipping cream (garnish)

Line a 9-inch square pan with aluminum foil, extending foil about 3 inches beyond top. Mix chocolate chips, water, gelatin and ½ cup brown sugar in a saucepan. Stir over low heat until gelatin is dissolved and chocolate chips are melted. Stir in egg yolks and orange juice; beat until light. Remove from heat. Beat egg whites until stiff but not dry; add salt. Beat remaining brown sugar into egg whites until they are glossy. Fold in chocolate mixture and whipped cream. Pour into pan. Refrigerate overnight. Next day lift soufflé by extended foil from pan; peel foil from sides. Cut into 2-inch squares. Place each square on serving dish. Make the following:

CHOCOLATE LEAVES

Makes 16 leaves

6 ounces (1 cup) semisweet
  chocolate chips, melted

1 tablespoon butter

Have ready a waxed-paper-lined 12 × 15-inch cookie sheet. Mix melted chocolate chips with butter until smooth. Spread mixture evenly on waxed paper; chill until firm. Invert waxed paper. Gently peel off waxed paper. Cut with sharp knife into leaf-shaped pieces about 2 × 1½-inches. Press a chocolate leaf onto each side of each square of Chocolate Soufflé. Garnish with whipped cream. Chill until ready to serve.

CHOCOLATE PRUNE SOUFFLÉ

Serve immediately from the oven.
Makes 8 to 10 servings

1 cup dried prunes, pitted
1¾ cups sugar
    Water to cover
½ cup cocoa

10 egg whites (room temperature)
1/16 teaspoon salt
½ cup whipping cream, whipped

Preheat oven to 300°. Butter a soufflé dish or tube pan. Combine prunes, ¾ cup sugar and water to cover in a saucepan; cook, stirring until sugar is dissolved. Cover pan; cook over low heat until prunes are tender and plump. Drain, reserving syrup. Purée prunes in blender. Combine cocoa and remaining sugar; mix together well. Beat egg whites with salt until frothy. Gradually add sugar-cocoa mixture, beating until egg whites are stiff. Thoroughly fold in puréed prunes. Place in soufflé dish or tube pan. Bake until raised and golden brown, about 45 minutes. Serve warm topped with whipped cream flavored with about 4 tablespoons of reserved syrup.

CHOCOLATE SOUFFLÉ

A classic, wonderful hot soufflé.
Makes 4 to 6 servings

3 tablespoons butter
3 tablespoons flour
¾ cup milk
2 teaspoons cornstarch
3 teaspoons water
4 egg yolks
⅓ cup sugar

1 teaspoon vanilla extract
2 ounces (2 squares) unsweetened
    chocolate
5 egg whites
2 tablespoons coffee
    Whipped cream (optional)

Preheat oven to 350°. Generously grease bottom and sides of an 8-inch soufflé dish and sprinkle with granulated sugar. Melt butter in saucepan. Add flour; stir until blended. Add milk, stirring constantly until thickened. Stir in cornstarch mixed with water. Bring to boil. Remove from heat; add egg yolks, which have been beaten with sugar, then add vanilla. Add chocolate, melted in coffee. Scrape the sauce into a large mixing bowl. Beat egg whites until stiff; scoop half into sauce and beat thoroughly with wire whisk. Fold in remaining egg whites. Scrape mixture into soufflé dish. Bake until well puffed and brown, 35 to 45 minutes. Serve at once. Top with sweetened whipped cream if desired.

FRENCH CHEF
CHOCOLATE SOUFFLÉ

A coffee-flavored version.
Makes 8 to 10 servings

½ cup sugar
⅓ cup cornstarch
1½ cups milk
4½ ounces (¾ cup) semisweet
    chocolate chips
½ teaspoon vanilla extract

3 tablespoons coffee
5 egg yolks, well beaten
7 egg whites
¼ teaspoon cream of tartar

Preheat oven to 325°. Generously grease a 2-quart soufflé dish. Mix sugar and cornstarch; add to milk. Melt chocolate chips and add to sugar mixture. Add vanilla, coffee and beaten egg yolks. Cook over boiling water until thick. Cool. Beat egg whites until stiff and gently fold in. Scrape mixture into soufflé dish. Bake until done, about 60 minutes.

ROSE'S CHOCOLATE SOUFFLÉ

Very rich, with a custardlike consistency.
Makes 10 to 12 servings

2½ ounces (2½ squares) unsweetened
    chocolate
2 cups milk
2 tablespoons butter

6 eggs, separated
7 tablespoons sugar
1½ tablespoons flour
1 teaspoon vanilla extract

Preheat oven to 350°. Grease a 2-quart soufflé dish well. Melt chocolate in double boiler over hot water. Heat milk to boiling; stir into chocolate. Add butter. Beat egg yolks with 6 tablespoons sugar and flour. Add egg yolk mixture to chocolate; cook until thick. Add vanilla. Let cool. Beat egg whites until stiff with remaining tablespoon of sugar; fold in chocolate mixture. Scrape into soufflé dish. Set soufflé dish in pan of water. Bake until set, about 60 minutes.

CHAPTER EIGHT

FROZEN DESSERTS

CHOCOLATE MINT ICE CREAM

Homemade chocolate ice cream with a kiss of mint.
Makes 4 to 6 servings

1 ounce (1 square) unsweetened
   chocolate, melted
⅔ cup sweetened condensed milk
⅔ cup water

¹⁄₁₆ teaspoon salt
⅔ cup whipping cream, whipped
½ teaspoon vanilla extract
½ teaspoon peppermint extract

Melt chocolate over hot water; add condensed milk. Cook 5 to 6 minutes until thick, stirring constantly. Add salt. Chill. Fold in whipped cream with vanilla and peppermint extracts. Pour into ice cube tray with freezer control set at highest point. Freeze to mush. Remove from tray; place in chilled bowl. Beat until smooth; return to tray. Freeze mixture until firm.

VELVETY
CHOCOLATE CHIP ICE CREAM

Molasses flavored—sensational!
Makes 5 to 6 servings

2 eggs, separated
⅔ cup sugar
¹⁄₁₆ teaspoon salt
½ cup chocolate-covered molasses
   chip candies, crushed

1½ cups milk
¼ cup water
2 tablespoons light corn syrup
1 teaspoon vanilla extract
½ cup whipping cream, whipped

Beat egg yolks; add ⅓ cup sugar, salt and crushed chocolate candy chips. Cook over hot water until mixture thickens, stirring constantly. Cool. Pour into 2 ice cube trays with freezer control at highest setting. Freeze to mush. Boil remaining sugar, water and syrup until small quantity dropped from tip of spoon spins a long thread. Beat egg whites until stiff; gradually add syrup mixture, beating constantly. Add vanilla. Cool. Place first mixture in chilled bowl; beat until smooth. Smooth in egg white mixture; fold in whipped cream. Return to tray; freeze until firm. Serve with chocolate sauce if desired.

CHOCOLATE ICE CREAM

Makes 4 servings

2 teaspoons unflavored gelatin
¼ cup cold water
2 ounces (2 squares) unsweetened
    chocolate
½ cup powdered sugar

1 cup milk
1/16 teaspoon salt
1½ teaspoons vanilla extract
1⅓ cups whipping cream, partially
    whipped

Soften gelatin in water 5 minutes. Melt chocolate over low heat. Add sugar; blend thoroughly. Gradually add milk. Bring to boiling point, stirring constantly. Remove from heat; add gelatin and salt. Chill in refrigerator until thick. Beat well with rotary beater. Add vanilla; fold in partially whipped cream. Pour into ice cube tray; place in freezer. Set freezer control at highest setting.

BRANDIED CHOCOLATE
PIE IN ICE CREAM SHELL

Makes one 8-inch pie

1 pint (block) peppermint ice cream
4 ounces sweet cooking chocolate
½ cup butter

¼ cup sugar
1½ teaspoons brandy flavoring
2 eggs

Line bottom of chilled 8-inch pie pan with ½-inch slices of ice cream; line sides with ¼-inch slices. Smooth ice cream with spoon to form shell, filling in with more ice cream where needed. Freeze until firm. Melt chocolate over low heat; cool. Using electric mixer, cream butter. Gradually blend in sugar, creaming well after each addition. Add cooled chocolate and brady flavoring; blend well. Add eggs one at a time, beating well. Continue beating until sugar is dissolved. Spoon into shell. Freeze until firm, 3 to 4 hours.

CHOCOLATE BISQUE CAPRI

Makes 16 servings

½ cup almonds, toasted and
   chopped
⅓ cup coconut, toasted and chopped

½ teaspoon almond extract
1 quart chocolate ice cream,
   softened

Combine almonds and coconut; reserve 2 tablespoons for topping. Quickly fold nuts and almond extract into softened ice cream. Place in small dessert cups; sprinkle with topping. Keep in freezer until ready to serve.

CHOCOLATE ICE CREAM CAKE

Makes 8 servings

1 (4½ ounces) package chocolate
   pudding mix
2 cups milk

1 sponge loaf cake
1 pint chocolate ice cream

Prepare chocolate pudding with milk according to directions on package. Cool. Slice sponge cake to fit bottom of ice cube tray. Pour pudding over, filling in any crevices. Slice ice cream; place on top of pudding. Place in freezing compartment. Let stand at least 1 hour with freezer control set at highest setting.

CHOCOLATE
SUPREME ICE CREAM PIE

A tender meringue crowning a rich ice cream pie.
Makes 8 to 10 servings

1 9-inch pie shell, baked
1 quart chocolate ice cream
2 egg whites

¼ cup powdered sugar
1 teaspoon vanilla extract

Preheat oven to 450°. Place ice cream in baked shell. Beat egg whites until very stiff. Add sugar and vanilla. Continue beating until meringue stands in peaks. Spread on top of ice cream. Brown slightly in oven. Serve immediately.

CHOCOLATE FRUIT POPS

Kids love these easy-to-make "pops."
Makes 10 pops

5 medium bananas or pears
10 wooden skewers
4½ ounces (¾ cup) semisweet
  chocolate chips

1 tablespoon butter
½ cup toasted nuts, chopped

Peel bananas or pears; cut in half crosswise. Insert skewer in cut end of each half. Wrap in foil; freeze. Melt chocolate and butter over hot water, blending until smooth. Spread mixture on frozen fruit. Roll in nuts. Serve at once or wrap in foil and return to freezer until ready to serve.

CHOCOLATE PRALINES BOMBE

Spectacular!
Makes 10 servings

PRALINES
  ¾ cup sugar
  ¾ cup almonds, slivered, chopped
    and toasted

CHOCOLATE CREAM CENTER
  1 quart ice cream, slightly softened
  ¼ cup canned chocolate-flavored
    syrup

Chocolate curls (optional)

CHOCOLATE SYRUP SAUCE
  ½ cup canned chocolate-flavored
    syrup
  ¾ cup sweetened condensed milk

For pralines, grease a sheet of heavy-duty aluminum foil. Melt sugar in saucepan over medium high heat, stirring constantly. Add slivered almonds. Continue stirring until almonds are coated with liquid and mixture is golden brown. Remove from heat at once. Pour onto aluminum foil. Cool. For chocolate cream center, whip ice cream. Gently fold in chocolate syrup. Covering with either a piece of heavy duty foil or lightweight clean towel, crush pralines with a mallet to a fine texture. Add pralines to cream mixture; blend well. Pour into large bowl. Cover and freeze. When chocolate cream is firmly frozen, unmold onto large dish. Spread the softened ice cream evenly over surface; return to freezer for hardening. Remove from freezer 10 to 15 minutes before serving. Garnish with chocolate curls. Cover with chocolate syrup sauce made by mixing the chocolate-flavored syrup and condensed milk together. Serve warm or cold over Chocolate Praline Bombe.

CHOCOLATE ICE CREAM PIE

A fluffy filling in an ice cream shell.
Makes 8 to 10 servings

1 pint (block) vanilla ice cream
4 ounces sweet cooking chocolate
½ cup butter

½ cup sugar
1 teaspoon vanilla extract
2 eggs

Chill an 8-inch pie pan. Line bottom with ½-inch slices of ice cream and sides with ¼-inch slices. Smooth ice cream with back of tablespoon to form shell; fill in where necessary with additional ice cream. Freeze until firm. Melt chocolate over low heat; cool. Cream butter and sugar together until light and fluffy. Add cooled chocolate and vanilla; blend again. Beat eggs in one at a time. Continue to beat until sugar is completely dissolved. Spread into ice cream shell. Freeze until firm.

CHOCOLATE
ICE CREAM SANDWICH

Makes 10 to 12 servings

1 quart (1 block) chocolate ice
cream
Graham crackers

Chocolate Banana Coating,
melted (see recipe, page 117)

Slice block of ice cream into bars about 3 × 3 inches. Sandwich ice cream between crackers. Freeze quickly. Coat with melted chocolate. Wrap individually. Freeze.

CHOCOLATE FROSTIE PIE

Makes one 9-inch pie

1 (14.5 ounces) package milk
chocolate frosting mix
1½ cups whipping cream
2 tablespoons hot water

1 tablespoon light corn syrup
1 cup nuts, finely chopped
½ teaspoon vanilla extract
1 9-inch pie shell, baked

Prepare 1 cup frosting mix as directed on package; set aside. Chill remaining frosting mix and whipping cream for 2 hours. Combine prepared frosting mix, water and corn syrup. Beat until smooth. Pour all but 1 tablespoon of corn syrup mixture into pie shell. Brush bottom and sides of pie shell; sprinkle with nuts. Beat cream-frosting mixture until stiff.

Spread in shell; drizzle reserved corn syrup mixture over top of pie. Draw spatula back and forth across top to marbleize. Place in freezer; freeze overnight. Let stand 10 to 15 minutes before serving.

·

CHOCOLATE ICE CREAM SURPRISE

Makes 6 servings

½ cup rice, uncooked
2 cups boiling water
½ teaspoon salt

¼ cup orange marmalade or apple jelly
1 pint chocolate ice cream

Rinse rice with cold water. Sprinkle into water which is boiling vigorously. Add salt; cover and boil until tender, about 20 minutes. Drain; cool slightly. Place a small mound on each serving plate. Top with heaping teaspoons of marmalade or jelly and heaping tablespoon of chocolate ice cream. Serve at once.

·

MOCHA BISQUE PIE

Makes one 9-inch pie

4 ounces (½ cup) marshmallows
½ cup water
1 teaspoon instant coffee
½ teaspoon salt
2 eggs, separated
¾ cup whipping cream, whipped
6 ounces (1 cup) semisweet
  chocolate chips

1 tablespoon butter
1 teaspoon vanilla extract
¼ teaspoon almond extract
1 cup brown sugar, firmly packed
1 9-inch pie shell, baked

Melt marshmallows, water, instant coffee and salt over medium heat, stirring constantly. Beat egg yolks slightly; add to mixture. Cook over medium heat about 1 minute, stirring constantly. Cool 10 to 15 minutes. Fold in whipped cream and freeze until firm. Combine chocolate chips and butter; melt over hot water. Beat egg whites until stiff but not dry; add vanilla and almond extracts, then brown sugar, beating until stiff and glossy. Place frozen mixture in chilled bowl; stir until smooth but not melted. Pour chocolate mixture over, in thin stream, stirring constantly to form "flecks" of melted chocolate. Fold in egg white mixture and pour into shell. Freeze until firm.

CHOCOLATE MINT FREEZE

Makes 12 servings

1 cup milk	½ teaspoon peppermint extract
1 cup marshmallows	½ teaspoon vanilla extract
2 cups whipping cream, whipped	2 cups chocolate wafers, finely
3 drops green food coloring	crushed

Dissolve marshmallows in hot milk; cool. Add whipped cream. Add coloring and vanilla and peppermint extracts. Sprinkle chocolate wafer crumbs in bottom of 2 ice cube trays; spoon mixture over crumbs. Top with thin layer of crumbs. Freeze until not quite solid, 4 to 5 hours. If made in advance thaw slightly just before serving.

CHOCOLATE MOCHA ICE CREAM PIE

Makes one 8- or 9-inch pie

¼ cup coffee, double strength	Chocolate Crumb Crust (see
1 pint chocolate ice cream	following recipe)

Add ¼ cup coffee to chocolate ice cream. Mix well. Spread in Chocolate Crumb Crust. Freeze several hours before serving.

CHOCOLATE CRUMB CRUST

Makes one 8- or 9-inch crust

1½ cups (about 30 wafers) chocolate	¼ cup butter
wafer crumbs	¼ cup sugar

Generously grease an 8- or 9-inch pie pan. Melt butter; add wafer crumbs and sugar. Combine well. Press crumb mixture into pie pan. Chill at least 5 minutes in coldest part of refrigerator.

CREAMY
CHOCOLATE FREEZER PIE

Lovely marbleized top; great for guests.
Makes one 9-inch pie

¾ *cup flour*
¼ *cup plus 2 tablespoons butter,*
   softened
⅓ *cup nuts, finely chopped*
 3 *tablespoons brown sugar*
 6 *ounces (1 cup) semisweet*
   chocolate chips

⅓ *cup cream cheese, softened*
¼ *cup sugar*
 2 *tablespoons milk*
⅛ *teaspoon salt*
 1 *envelope dessert topping mix*
 2 *tablespoons butter*

Preheat oven to 425°. Mix flour, butter (reserving 2 tablespoons), nuts and brown sugar. Mix until crumbly. Press into sides and bottom of 9-inch pie pan; place 8-inch pie pan firmly inside. Place in oven. Bake 15 minutes. Remove from oven; remove 8-inch pie pan. Cool. Melt ¾ cup chocolate chips over hot water; cool. Blend melted chocolate, cream cheese, sugar, milk and salt at top speed of electric mixer. Prepare topping mix as directed on package. Fold into cream cheese mixture. Pour into baked crust. Make syrup by melting 2 tablespoons butter and ¼ cup chocolate chips; drizzle over top. Marbleize top by drawing spatula back and forth across top. Freeze until firm. Remove from freezer about 15 minutes before serving.

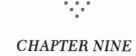

CHAPTER NINE

CONFECTIONS

QUICK FUDGE BALLS

Makes 32 pieces

3 envelopes (1 ounce) liquid
   unsweetened chocolate
¼ cup butter, softened
½ teaspoon vanilla extract
¼ teaspoon almond extract

⅛ teaspoon salt
2 cups powdered sugar, sifted
1 tablespoon whipping cream
½ cup nuts, very finely chopped

Mix first five ingredients well. Gradually blend in powdered sugar, alternating with cream. Roll mixture into balls, using about 1 tablespoon for each ball. Roll balls in nuts.

NUT CHOCOLATE BALLS

Makes 32 pieces

6 ounces (1 cup) semisweet
   chocolate chips
½ cup nuts, chopped
⅛ teaspoon salt
½ cup sour cream

1 tablespoon butter, softened
1 tablespoon prepared cocoa
1 tablespoon rum flavoring
1 teaspoon water
¼ cup powdered sugar, sifted

Melt chocolate over hot water; remove from heat. Stir in nuts, 1/16 teaspoon salt and sour cream; chill until firm. Mix remaining ingredients well until crumbly. Form chocolate mixture into small balls about 1-inch round; roll in crumb mix. Chill until ready to serve.

DIVINE NUTTY FUDGE

Makes about 3 dozen pieces

4 ounces (4 squares) unsweetened
   chocolate, grated
½ cup butter
2 cups powdered sugar
1 egg, beaten

¼ cup sweetened condensed milk
½ teaspoon black walnut flavoring
½ teaspoon vanilla extract
2 cups nuts, finely chopped

Lightly grease an 8- or 9-inch square pan. Melt chocolate and butter together in top of double boiler, stirring until melted. Cool. Beat powdered sugar, egg, black walnut flavoring, milk and vanilla extract together. Add to chocolate mixture. Add nuts. Place in pan. Refrigerate overnight. Cut into 1½-inch squares.

MAMIE EISENHOWER'S FUDGE

This recipe was given to me by Ike's niece.
Makes 5 pounds

4½ cups sugar
2 tablespoons butter
1/16 teaspoon salt
1 (12 ounces) can evaporated milk
9 ounces (1½ cups) semisweet chocolate chips

12 ounces sweet cooking chocolate, broken
2 cups marshmallow cream
2 cups walnuts or pecans, chopped

Grease a 9 × 13 × 2-inch pan. Combine sugar, butter, salt and milk in large saucepan. Bring to a boil over medium heat. Boil 5 to 6 minutes, stirring constantly. Combine chocolate, marshmallow cream and nuts in a bowl; pour hot mixture over this until chocolate is melted. Place in pan. Refrigerate until cool. Cut into squares when cool. Store in airtight container.

•

CHERRY NUT FUDGE

Great holiday fudge.
Makes 3 dozen pieces

1/16 teaspoon salt
1¼ cups evaporated milk
2½ cups sugar
12 ounces (2 cups) semisweet chocolate chips

½ teaspoon vanilla extract
¼ teaspoon almond extract
12 maraschino cherries
24 pecans, halved
1½ tablespoons butter

Grease well a 9-inch square pan. Mix first three ingredients in large saucepan. Bring to boil; boil 5 minutes, stirring constantly. Add 1½ cups chocolate chips and vanilla and almond extracts; stir until chocolate chips are melted. Pour into pan. Cut cherries in half, drain and dry well. Press cherries and nuts gently into mixture in even rows. Heat ½ cup chocolate chips and butter until completely melted; pour over fudge, being sure cherries and nuts are completely coated. Chill until firm, about 4 hours. Cut into squares so that a cherry or nut is centered on each piece.

•

VELVET LEAPS

Makes 5 dozen pieces

12 ounces (2 cups) semisweet
    chocolate chips
½ cup sour cream
¾ cup powdered sugar

¼ teaspoon salt
2 teaspoons rum flavoring
2 cups fine vanilla wafer crumbs

Melt chocolate chips in top of double boiler over hot, not boiling, water. Remove from heat; stir in sour cream, powdered sugar, salt and rum flavoring. Blend in crumbs. Dust hands with powdered sugar; shape mixture into 1-inch balls. Chill until firm.

Variation: Press a whole pecan into top of each ball before chilling.

.

BUTTERSCOTCH CHOCOLATE FUDGE

I love the buttery taste of butterscotch in fudge.
Makes about 5 dozen pieces

6 ounces (1 cup) butterscotch chips
6 ounces (1 cup) semisweet
    chocolate chips
½ cup sour cream
¼ teaspoon salt

¾ cup powdered sugar, sifted
1 teaspoon grated orange peel
2 cups vanilla wafers, finely
    crushed
½ cup nuts, toasted

Line an 8-inch square pan with waxed paper. Melt butterscotch and chocolate chips over hot water until melted. Remove from heat; stir in next four ingredients. When well mixed, blend in crumbs. Press mixture into pan. Sprinkle and press nuts on top; chill until firm, 4 to 5 hours. Cut into squares.

.

GOOD OL' FASHIONED FUDGE

Dates are the secret of this popular fudge.
Makes 2½ dozen pieces

3 ounces (3 squares) unsweetened
    chocolate, melted
1½ cups condensed milk
2 tablespoons butter

1 tablespoon vanilla extract
2 cups powdered sugar, sifted
½ cup dates, finely chopped
½ cup nuts, finely chopped

Butter well an 8-inch square pan. Melt chocolate in double boiler over hot water. Add condensed milk; cook 5 minutes, stirring until mixture thickens. Remove from heat; add butter and vanilla. Sift in sugar; blend thoroughly. Fold in dates and nuts. Place in pan. Chill 4 hours; cut into squares.

■

BAKED FUDGE

Very quick and creamy.
Makes 3 dozen pieces

1 cup canned chocolate frosting
2 eggs

1 cup cream cheese, softened
1 teaspoon vanilla extract

Preheat oven to 375°. Grease an 8-inch square pan. Blend all ingredients thoroughly. Beat at highest speed of electric mixer until cream cheese is smooth, about 1 minute. Place in pan. Bake until fudge shrinks from edge of pan, about 45 minutes. Refrigerate 3 to 4 hours. Cut into squares.

■

LUKE'S FUDGE

Pure, rich, fudge.
Makes about 2½ dozen pieces

1 cup sugar
1 cup brown sugar, firmly packed
¾ cup milk
2 tablespoons light corn syrup

2 ounces (2 squares) unsweetened
chocolate
3 tablespoons butter
1 teaspoon vanilla extract

Grease well an 8 × 8 × 2-inch pan. Combine sugars, milk and syrup in a saucepan. Add chocolate; cook slowly, stirring until mixture boils. Boil slowly, stirring occasionally, until a small quantity dropped into cold water forms a soft ball. Remove from heat; add butter; cool to lukewarm. Add vanilla; beat until thick. Pour into pan. Cool; cut into squares.

■

FUDGY CREAM CHEESE FUDGE

Makes 1 pound

1 (3 ounce) package cream cheese, softened
1 tablespoon whipping cream
2 cups powdered sugar
2 ounces (2 squares) unsweetened chocolate, melted

½ teaspoon vanilla extract
1/16 teaspoon salt
1 cup nuts, chopped

Grease an 8-inch square pan. Mix cream cheese and whipping cream; beat until smooth. Gradually beat in sugar. Add melted chocolate, blending well. Stir in last three ingredients. Press into pan; chill until firm. Cut into squares.

PEANUT BUTTER FUDGE

Unbearably good!
Makes 1½ pounds

6 ounces (1 cup) butterscotch chips
6 ounces (1 cup) semisweet chocolate chips

½ cup chunky peanut butter
⅔ cup sweetened condensed milk

Grease well an 8-inch square pan. Mix butterscotch and chocolate chips and peanut butter in top of double boiler; place over hot water until bits melt. Stir until blended. Carefully stir in condensed milk until just blended. Spread mixture into pan; chill until firm. Cut into squares.

CHOCOLATE PEANUT CLUSTERS

Makes 2 dozen pieces

6 ounces (1 cup) semisweet chocolate chips

1 tablespoon butter
¾ cup peanuts, shelled

Melt chocolate and butter over hot water; stir well. Add peanuts; stir. Drop by teaspoonfuls onto waxed paper. Cool.

CHOCOLATE PECANS

Makes about 10 dozen

3½ cups pecans
½ teaspoon salt
6 tablespoons sugar

3 tablespoons instant chocolate
drink mix

Preheat oven to 350°. Cover nuts with hot water; drain and place in a bowl. Sprinkle with a mixture of sugar and salt. Add chocolate and stir until nuts are well coated, about 10 minutes. Separate and place on waxed paper. Refrigerate until firm.

CHOCOLATE PUFFED RICE CANDIES

Makes 3 dozen pieces

12 ounces (2 cups) semisweet
chocolate chips
½ teaspoon vanilla extract

4 cups puffed rice cereal
⅔ cup coconut, shredded
2 cups miniature marshmallows

Preheat oven to 350°. Melt chocolate over hot, but not boiling, water; stir in vanilla. Toast puffed rice in a shallow baking pan about 10 minutes; pour into well-greased bowl. Add ⅓ cup coconut. Pour melted chocolate over puffed rice and stir until evenly coated; stir in marshmallows until coated. Press mixture into a 9-inch square pan. Sprinkle with rest of coconut; press down lightly. Chill in refrigerator several hours; cut into squares.

CHOCOLATE SUMMITS

Makes 3 to 4 dozen pieces

½ cup evaporated milk
¾ cup sugar
2 tablespoons butter
4½ ounces (¾ cup) semisweet
chocolate chips

1 teaspoon vanilla extract
2 cups Cheerios®
1 cup salted peanuts
1 cup pretzel sticks, broken

Combine evaporated milk, sugar and butter in medium saucepan; bring to a full boil, stirring constantly. Continue to boil and stir for 2 minutes. Remove from heat. Add chocolate chips and vanilla; stir until mixture is smooth. Combine cereal, peanuts and pretzels; add chocolate mixture; toss lightly until well coated. Drop quickly by heaping teaspoonfuls onto waxed paper. Let stand until set.

CHOCOLATE TOUCHDOWNS

Makes 6 dozen pieces

4 ounces (⅔ cup) semisweet
   chocolate chips
2 tablespoons butter
¼ teaspoon cinnamon

⅛ teaspoon nutmeg
72 Spoon-Size Shredded Wheat
   cereal

Melt chocolate chips and butter together; add cinnamon and nutmeg, mixing well. Coat each piece of shredded wheat cereal with mixture. Place on waxed paper; let stand until chocolate hardens.

·

CHOCOLATE TRUFFLES

Nothing is better than dense, homemade truffles.
Makes ½ pound

4½ ounces (¾ cup) semisweet
   chocolate chips
⅓ cup plus 1 tablespoon sweetened
   condensed milk

1/16 teaspoon salt
½ teaspoon vanilla extract
½ teaspoon almond extract

Grease and line with waxed paper an 8 × 8 × 2-inch pan. Melt chocolate in top of double boiler over rapidly boiling water; do not stir. Remove from heat; add condensed milk, salt and vanilla and almond extracts. Stir until blended. Turn into pan and press into a block about 1-inch high. Chill several hours until firm. Remove waxed paper. Cut into squares.

·

CONNIE'S FONDANT

Make your own freshly dipped chocolates.
Makes 40 to 45 centers for dipping

2 cups sugar
1/16 teaspoon salt
1 tablespoon light corn syrup
½ cup whipping cream
¼ cup milk
1 teaspoon vanilla extract

3 ounces (3 squares) unsweetened
   chocolate, melted
3 teaspoons water
   Chocolate for dipping (see box,
   page 194)

Combine first 5 ingredients in large saucepan; heat, stirring well until sugar is dissolved and mixture boils. Cook 2 to 3 minutes covered, without stirring, then remove cover;

continue cooking until a small amount dropped from a spoon into cold water forms a soft ball. Wipe sides of pan with cloth dampened and wrapped around fork to remove the sugar crystals. Pour fondant onto a cold platter which has been moistened; spread to about ¼-inch thickness. Cool until lukewarm, then work with a wooden spoon until creamy white by lifting and folding from edges to center. Continue to work and knead until smooth; blend in vanilla. Cool, uncovered. Wrap in waxed paper; place in tin or plastic box and cover tightly. Place in refrigerator. Chill at least 24 hours. To dip, remove from refrigerator and divide into two parts. Knead briefly. If you wish, add food coloring, chopped nuts or bits of candied orange peel. Form each half into a roll 1 inch in diameter. Slice into ½-inch rounds. Shape rounds into ovals or rectangles. Let stand until it reaches room temperature before dipping.

■

DARK CHOCOLATE NUT CANDIES

Makes 2 pounds

9 ounces (1½ cups) semisweet
    chocolate chips
1½ cups nuts, finely chopped
1½ cups powdered sugar, sifted

1 egg white
2 tablespoons rum
1 tablespoon butter
¾ cup sweetened condensed milk

Grease an 8-inch square pan. Melt chocolate in top of double boiler over boiling water. Combine nuts, sugar, egg white and rum; mix well. Stir condensed milk and butter into warm chocolate; cook until thick, 6 to 7 minutes. Cool. Place nut mixture in pan; pour chocolate mixture over. Cool. Cut into squares.

■

PERK-UPS

Makes 32 pieces

12 ounces (2 cups) semisweet
    chocolate chips
¾ cup sweetened condensed milk

1 teaspoon vanilla extract
1½ cups walnuts, chopped

Melt chocolate chips over simmering water. Remove from heat. Stir in condensed milk, vanilla, and ½ cup chopped walnuts; mix well. Chill until firm enough to handle. Divide mixture in half. Shape each half into a roll about 1½ inches in diameter. Coat each roll with ½ cup of remaining chopped walnuts. Cut each roll into 16 slices.

■

DIPPING CHOCOLATE

Dipping candy is an art. If you would like to be proficient at it, you will need to know a few of the basic rules.

Be sure you do your dipping in a well-ventilated room that is free of drafts and steam. You may use any semisweet dipping chocolate. Start with about 16 ounces; do not use more than 2 pounds at a time. Melt it in the top of a double boiler over hot water (never boiling). When it reaches 130°F on a candy thermometer, remove the top of the double boiler. Replace the hot water in the bottom of the double boiler with cold water and heat it. Place the top of the double boiler back on top of the cold water and stir the chocolate quickly with a circular motion, scraping the sides often, which will help reduce the temperature to 83°. Remove the top of the double boiler and add warm water to the bottom until the water temperature reaches 85°. Remove the thermometer; put the chocolate back on top of the water. You will need to work rapidly. Drop the food to be coated into the chocolate and stir well with a two-tined metal fork until completely coated. Lift the food out by slipping a fork underneath each piece. Tap each dipped piece on the rim of the pan several times. Draw it across the rim to remove any excess chocolate. Invert the dipped pieces onto a wire rack that has been covered with waxed paper. Let the pieces stand 5 to 6 minutes, then remove them.

ROCKY ROAD CHOCOLATE BARS

Quick and foolproof.
Makes 1½ dozen pieces

40 miniature marshmallows
¾ cup walnuts, chopped

8 ounces sweet chocolate, melted
½ teaspoon black walnut flavoring

Line bottom of 9 × 5-inch loaf pan with waxed paper; extend paper 2 inches above top at either end. Place marshmallows and nuts alternately on bottom of pan, leaving spaces between each. Melt chocolate in top of double boiler over boiling water until partially melted; remove from boiling water. Stir until completely melted; add black walnut flavoring and beat well. Pour over contents in pan, distributing chocolate with fork. Tap pan a few times to settle chocolate. Cool until hardened. When ready to serve, run sharp knife around sides of pan; remove candy with paper ends. Cut into 1 × 2-inch bars.

QUICK CHOCOLATE DATE CANDIES

Makes 2 dozen pieces

6 ounces (1 cup) semisweet
  chocolate chips
1 tablespoon water

3 tablespoons light corn syrup
1¼ cups dates, finely chopped

Place waxed paper on a cookie sheet. Heat chocolate chips, water and syrup together over hot water. Remove from heat when chocolate is melted; stir in dates carefully. When well mixed, spread on waxed paper. Chill until firm. Break into pieces.

•

QUICK CHOCOLATE RAISIN BRAN CANDY

Crunchy and delicious.
Makes 3 dozen pieces

6 ounces (1 cup) semisweet
  chocolate chips
1 tablespoon water

3 tablespoons light corn syrup
2 cups raisin bran

Place waxed paper on a cookie sheet. Heat chocolate chips, water and corn syrup together over hot water. Remove from heat when chocolate is melted. Stir in raisin bran. Drop by teaspoonfuls onto waxed paper. Chill until firm.

•

MOM'S CHOCOLATE CANDY

Makes about 33

2 egg whites
½ cup sugar
4½ ounces (¾ cup) semisweet
  chocolate chips, melted

1 cup nuts, chopped

Preheat oven to 325°. Grease and lightly flour a cookie sheet. Beat whites until stiff. Gradually add sugar; beat again. Add chocolate chips and nuts. Drop by ½ teaspoonfuls, leaving a space between each (five across on a large cookie sheet). Bake until brown, 15 to 20 minutes. Remove from cookie sheet while cookies are warm.

MARSHMALLOW
BUTTERSCOTCH CHOCOLATE CANDY

Makes 3 to 4 dozen pieces

6 ounces (1 cup) semisweet
   chocolate chips
6 ounces (1 cup) butterscotch chips

2 cups large marshmallows,
   quartered, or miniatures
1 cup nuts, chopped

Line an 8-inch square pan with aluminum foil. Melt chocolate and butterscotch chips over hot water; add marshmallows and nuts. Spread in pan; chill until firm. Cut into squares.

·

CHOCOLATE
MARSHMALLOW SQUARES

Makes 3 dozen pieces

12 ounces (2 cups) semisweet
   chocolate chips
2 tablespoons butter

3 cups marshmallows, cut into
   quarters, or miniatures
2 cups pretzels, broken

Line a 9-inch square pan with aluminum foil. Melt chocolate chips and butter over hot water. Remove from heat; add marshmallows and pretzels. Fold until well blended. Spread mixture evenly in pan; refrigerate until firm. Allow to stand at room temperature a few minutes before removing from pan to cut into squares.

·

CHOCOLATE NUT CLUSTERS

Makes 1½ dozen pieces

½ cup coconut, flaked
½ cup nuts, finely chopped
½ cup nuts, coarsely chopped
6 ounces (1 cup) semisweet
   chocolate chips

½ teaspoon vanilla extract
1 cup mixed dried fruit, chopped

Place a piece of waxed paper on large cookie sheet. Sprinkle with coconut and finely chopped nuts. Melt chocolate in top of double boiler over hot water; remove when melted. Stir in coarsely chopped nuts, vanilla extract and dried fruit. Drop chocolate mixture by teaspoonfuls onto coconut-nut mixture and roll until well coated. Chill until firm.

CHOCOLATE-COFFEE-COCONUT CANDIES

Makes about 4 dozen pieces

2 tablespoons instant coffee
2 tablespoons butter
⅓ cup water
1½ cups brown sugar, firmly packed
1½ cups coconut

6 ounces (1 cup) semisweet chocolate chips
¼ teaspoon almond extract
½ teaspoon vanilla extract
¼ teaspoon black walnut flavoring

Line a cookie sheet with waxed paper. Mix together first five ingredients; cook over medium heat, stirring constantly. When sugar is dissolved, bring mixture to a boil; boil 1 minute. Remove from heat. Add chocolate chips; stir until melted. Stir in almond and vanilla extracts and black walnut flavoring. Drop mixture by teaspoonfuls onto cookie sheet. Chill until firm.

VERMONT TOFFEE

Makes 3 to 4 pounds

1 cup butter
1 cup sugar
1 tablespoon light corn syrup

3 tablespoons water
1 cup almonds, finely chopped
6 ounces milk chocolate

Heavily grease an 8- or a 9-inch square pan. Combine first four ingredients in heavy saucepan. Bring to a boil; stir until sugar dissolves. Cook over medium heat until candy thermometer registers 260°. When candy begins to turn dark on sides of pan, lower heat and continue to cook, stirring constantly to prevent scorching, until thermometer registers 290°. Add ½ cup almonds and cook, stirring constantly, until thermometer reaches 300°. Pour into pan. Cool thoroughly. Remove from pan. Melt ½ of chocolate; stir in ½ remaining almonds. Spread over one side of the toffee. Let cool. Turn over. Melt remaining chocolate; pour over uncoated side. Sprinkle with remaining almonds. Cool thoroughly. Break into chunks. Place in waxed paper; refrigerate overnight.

QUICK
CHOCOLATY PRETZEL STICKS

Makes 2 to 2½ dozen pieces

6 ounces (1 cup) semisweet
   chocolate chips
1 tablespoon water

3 tablespoons light corn syrup
2 cups whole pretzel sticks

Place waxed paper on a cookie sheet. Heat chocolate chips, water and corn syrup together over hot water. Remove from heat when chocolate is melted. Stir in pretzels, carefully, so as not to break. When well mixed, spread on waxed paper. Chill until firm.

CHOCOLATE NUT BRITTLE

Makes 2 pounds

2 tablespoons water
1½ cups butter
1 tablespoon instant coffee
2 cups sugar

2 cups nuts, halved and toasted
½ teaspoon almond extract
6 ounces (1 cup) semisweet
   chocolate chips

Grease a large sheet of heavy-duty aluminum foil. Mix first four ingredients in deep saucepan. Cook over medium heat, stirring constantly. Bring to full boil; continue boiling about 8 minutes, stirring from bottom often. Remove from heat; stir in 1½ cup nuts and almond extract. Spread at once on foil; cool completely. Melt chocolate chips over hot water; spread over cooled candy. Finely chop remaining nuts and sprinkle on top. Cool completely. Break into pieces.

CHOCOLATE MINT CLUSTERS

Makes 1½ dozen pieces

½ cup peppermint candy
6 ounces (1 cup) semisweet
   chocolate chips

½ cup instant powdered milk
1 cup nuts, finely chopped

Finely crush candy with rolling pin. Place chocolate in bowl over hot water, over low heat, until chocolate melts. Remove bowl from water; stir in powdered milk and nuts. Drop by teaspoonfuls onto the crushed candy. Turn clusters constantly to be sure to coat completely. Remove and place on waxed paper. Chill until firm.

CHOCOLATE ORIENTAL DROPS

Makes 48 pieces

4½ ounces (¾ cup) semisweet
    chocolate chips
¾ cup caramels

1 (3 ounces) can chow mein noodles
1 cup salted peanuts

Melt chocolate and caramels in the top of double boiler over hot water. Remove from heat; stir in noodles and peanuts. Mix well. Drop by teaspoonfuls onto waxed paper. Chill.

CHOCOLATE BUTTER CRUNCH

The buttery flavor and crunchy texture make this irresistible.
Makes 1 pound

1 cup milk chocolate, shaved
1 cup butter

1½ cups sugar
1½ cups nuts, finely chopped

Grease well an 8 × 8 × 2-inch pan. Melt butter in large skillet; add sugar. Cook, stirring constantly, over medium heat until blended; add nuts. Pour into pan. Sprinkle with chocolate and allow to melt slightly; spread evenly. Cool. Break into desired number of pieces.

CHOCOLATE BITES

Bars with a delicious butterscotch and chocolate covering.
Makes 4 dozen pieces

1 cup maple syrup
½ cup sugar
½ cup brown sugar, firmly packed
1 cup peanut butter

6 cups corn flakes
6 ounces (1 cup) butterscotch chips
6 ounces (1 cup) semisweet
    chocolate chips

Mix first three ingredients in large saucepan. Bring just to a boil over medium heat. Stir in peanut butter; remove from heat. Carefully add corn flakes so as not to break into smaller flakes. Press into large baking pan. Combine butterscotch and chocolate chips over hot water. Place over mixture in pan. Chill until firm. Cut into bars.

CARAMEL NUT CHOCOLATES

Makes 2½ pounds

1 cup brown sugar, firmly packed
1 cup sugar
1 cup light corn syrup
1 cup sweetened condensed milk
½ cup whipping cream
1 cup milk

6 ounces (6 squares) unsweetened chocolate, melted
2 tablespoons butter
2½ teaspoons vanilla extract
⅛ teaspoon salt
2 cups nuts, finely chopped

Grease well an 8 × 8 × 2-inch pan. Combine sugars, corn syrup, condensed milk, whipping cream and milk. Cook slowly until sugars are dissolved. Melt chocolate over hot water; add butter. Stir into first mixture. Cook slowly, stirring constantly until a small amount dropped in cold water forms a firm ball. Remove from heat; add remaining ingredients. Pour into pan; cool. Cut in squares. Wrap separately in waxed paper.

BUTTERSCOTCH CHOCOLATE CANDIES

Chow mein noodles add just the right texture.
Makes 3 dozen pieces

6 ounces (1 cup) butterscotch chips
6 ounces (1 cup) semisweet chocolate chips

3 cups chow mein noodles
1 cup nuts (optional)

Grease a 9-inch square pan. Melt butterscotch and chocolate chips over hot water. Stir in noodles, and nuts if desired. Press into pan; chill until set. Cut into squares.

CHAPTER TEN

SAUCES
AND FONDUES

Sauces

SACRAMENTO CHOCOLATE SAUCE

The perfect accompaniment for ice cream.
Makes 2½ cups

¼ cup unsalted butter
1¼ cups sweetened condensed milk
6 ounces (1 cup) semisweet
  chocolate chips

1 teaspoon vanilla extract
½ teaspoon almond extract
¼ cup water

Mix butter and condensed milk in saucepan. Bring to boil over medium heat, stirring constantly for 1 minute. Remove from heat; add chocolate chips and vanilla and almond extracts. Stir until smooth and well blended, gradually adding water.

CHOCOLATE HARD SAUCE

Try this on Brown Betty.
Makes about 1⅓ cups

1 tablespoon whipping cream
1 teaspoon cocoa

½ cup butter, softened
1 cup powdered sugar, sifted

Mix first three ingredients until light and fluffy. Slowly beat in powdered sugar.

EASY CHOCOLATE SAUCE

Makes about 1¼ cups

6 ounces (1 cup) semisweet
  chocolate chips
½ cup milk

¼ cup light corn syrup
½ teaspoon vanilla or almond
  extract

Combine chocolate chips, milk and corn syrup in a small saucepan. Cook over medium heat, stirring constantly until chocolate is melted and mixture is smooth. Remove from heat; stir in vanilla or almond extract. Cool at room temperature.

WONDERFUL SAUCE

Honey and peanut butter make this a truly wonderful sauce.
Makes 1¼ cups

½ cup chocolate syrup
½ cup honey
¼ cup evaporated milk

½ cup chunky peanut butter
1 teaspoon vanilla extract

Mix all ingredients in small saucepan; cook over low heat until smooth, stirring constantly. Serve warm.

·

CHOCOLATE HONEY SAUCE

Makes about 1½ cups

¼ cup honey
¼ cup water

6 ounces (1 cup) semisweet
chocolate chips

Mix all ingredients over hot water until melted.

·

CHOCOLATE MARSHMALLOW SAUCE

Buttery and thick.
Makes about 3 cups

½ cup butter
½ cup milk
¹⁄₁₆ teaspoon salt
6 ounces (1 cup) semisweet
chocolate chips

½ teaspoon vanilla extract
½ teaspoon almond extract
1 (7½ ounces) jar marshmallow
cream

Bring butter, milk and salt to a boil over medium heat, stirring constantly. Remove from heat. Add chocolate chips and vanilla and almond extracts, stirring until well blended. Slowly beat in marshmallow cream.

·

CHOCOLATE SAUCE

A classic chocolate sauce for cakes, puddings and ice cream.
Makes about 1 cup

1 envelope (1 ounce) premelted
unsweetened chocolate
or
1 square (1 ounce) unsweetened
chocolate
or
¼ cup unsweetened cocoa

¼ cup water
¾ cup light corn syrup
Dash salt
½ teaspoon vanilla extract
3 tablespoons evaporated milk or
half-and-half

Combine chocolate or cocoa and water in small saucepan; stir over low heat until mixture is smooth. Add corn syrup and salt; mix well. Simmer 10 to 12 minutes, stirring frequently. Remove pan from heat. Stir in vanilla and evaporated milk or half-and-half. Refrigerate until very cold. Serve in chilled pitcher.

COFFEE-CHOCOLATE SAUCE

Makes about 1¼ cups

8 ounces sweet chocolate
½ cup coffee, strong

¼ cup wine or rum

Melt chocolate and coffee together over hot water; stir until smooth. Before serving add wine or rum.

HOT FUDGE
MARSHMALLOW SAUCE

Makes 3 cups

6 ounces (1 cup) semisweet
chocolate chips
1 cup evaporated milk

1 cup marshmallows, cut in
quarters
1 teaspoon vanilla extract

Combine chocolate chips, milk and marshmallows in a saucepan over low heat. Cook, stirring constantly, until chocolate and marshmallows are melted. Add vanilla. Serve warm.

FRUIT CHOCOLATE SAUCE

Makes about ¾ cup

2 ounces (2 squares) unsweetened
   chocolate
2 tablespoons sugar

¼ cup whipping cream
¼ cup raspberry jam
1 tablespoon wine

Mix all ingredients in top of double boiler. Cook over hot water, stirring constantly until mixture is smooth.

FUDGY BROWN SUGAR SAUCE

Makes 2 cups

2 ounces (⅓ cup) semisweet
   chocolate chips
¼ cup butter
1½ cups brown sugar, firmly packed

¹⁄₁₆ teaspoon salt
¾ cup evaporated milk
1 teaspoon vanilla extract

Mix first four ingredients in a saucepan; cook over medium heat, stirring constantly until thoroughly blended. Gradually add evaporated milk. Bring to full boil, stirring constantly. Remove from heat; stir in vanilla. Serve warm or cold.

HOT FUDGE SAUCE

Makes 2 cups

2⅓ squares (2⅓ ounces) unsweetened
   chocolate, grated
⅔ cup Mocha Mix
1 cup sugar

¹⁄₁₆ teaspoon salt
1 tablespoon butter
½ teaspoon vanilla extract

Mix chocolate with a little Mocha Mix in top of double boiler until smooth. Stir in remaining Mocha Mix. Cook over low heat, stirring until mixture begins to boil. Add sugar and salt; cook until granules dissolve, stirring constantly. Remove double boiler from heat; add butter and vanilla. Keep warm until needed.

SPECIAL NUT FUDGE SAUCE

Makes about 2 cups

⅓ cup sweetened condensed milk
⅓ cup water
½ teaspoon vanilla extract
½ teaspoon almond extract

6 ounces (1 cup) semisweet
   chocolate chips
½ cup nuts, finely chopped

Mix milk, water and vanilla and almond extracts. Melt chocolate chips over hot water. Stir into first mixture. Add nuts. Serve warm.

PEANUT BUTTER CHOCOLATE SAUCE

Makes 2¼ cups

½ cup peanut butter
6 ounces (1 cup) semisweet
   chocolate chips

1/16 teaspoon salt
¾ cup whipping cream

Melt peanut butter, chocolate chips and salt over hot water. Blend in whipping cream.

QUICK CHOCOLATE SOUR CREAM SAUCE

Makes about 3 cups

1 cup sour cream
1 tablespoon water
⅛ teaspoon salt
6 ounces (1 cup) semisweet
   chocolate chips, melted

1 cup marshmallows, cut in
   quarters

Blend sour cream, water and salt into melted chocolate chips; fold in marshmallows.

QUICK SAUCE

Makes ¾ cup

½ cup cocoa
1/16 teaspoon salt

1 tablespoon boiling water
¼ cup light corn syrup

Mix cocoa, salt and water until well blended; stir in corn syrup.

·

QUEENLY CHOCOLATE SAUCE

Makes 1 cup

2 ounces (2 squares) unsweetened
   chocolate
6 tablespoons water
½ cup sugar

1/16 teaspoon salt
3 tablespoons butter
½ teaspoon vanilla extract
½ teaspoon almond extract

Melt chocolate in water in saucepan over very low heat; blend. Add sugar and salt. Cook until sugar is dissolved and mixture is slightly thick, stirring constantly. Add butter and vanilla and almond extracts.

Fondues

TAMMY'S CHOCOLATE FONDUE

Makes about 1 cup

2 ounces (⅓ cup) semisweet
   chocolate chips
½ cup whipping cream

2 tablespoons orange liqueur
½ teaspoon vanilla extract

Slowly melt chocolate with cream, stirring constantly and being careful not to scorch. When mixed, add orange liqueur and vanilla; stir until well blended. Keep warm over low heat. Serve as a dip for any of the following: apples, bananas, cherries, oranges, peaches, pears, pineapple, strawberries or, if you prefer, angel food cake, chiffon cake, ladyfingers, pound cake or sponge cake.

EASY CHOCOLATE FONDUE

Fondue in minutes.

1 cup canned chocolate frosting
½ cup miniature marshmallows

½ teaspoon vanilla extract

Place frosting over low heat in medium saucepan; stir in marshmallows. Continue stirring until marshmallows are melted and well blended, 5 to 6 minutes. Add vanilla; mix well. Keep warm over low heat.

CHOCOLATE-ORANGE FONDUE

Makes 3 cups

12 ounces (2 cups) semisweet
chocolate chips
1 cup evaporated milk
¼ cup unsalted butter

1 cup orange-flavored liqueur
½ teaspoon almond extract
½ teaspoon vanilla extract
24 ladyfingers

Mix all ingredients over low heat; cook until chocolate is melted, stirring constantly. Serve as a dip for ladyfingers. Keep warm over low heat.

CHOCOLATE FONDUE CAFÉ

Makes 3 cups

¾ cup American cheese, shredded
¼ cup flour
1 tablespoon cocoa
1 cup cream cheese, softened

⅔ cup brown sugar, firmly packed
2 cups hot coffee
24 ladyfingers

Blend American cheese and flour. Blend cocoa, cream cheese and sugar separately. Heat coffee in fondue pot slowly; stir in both cheese mixtures. When very smooth and dipping consistency, serve as dip for ladyfingers. Keep hot over low heat.

INDEX